Also by Julie Morgenstern

Organizing from the Inside Out

Time Management from the Inside Out

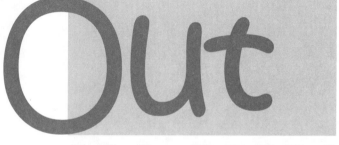

Organizing

FROM THE

Inside

Out

FOR TEENS

Organizing FROM THE Inside Out

FOR TEENS

**The Foolproof System
for Organizing Your Room,
Your Time, and Your Life**

Julie Morgenstern and
Jessi Morgenstern-Colón

Illustrations by Janet Pedersen

AN OWL BOOK

HENRY HOLT AND COMPANY • NEW YORK

Henry Holt and Company, LLC
Publishers since 1866
115 West 18th Street
New York, New York 10011

Library of Congress Cataloging-in-Publication Data

Morgenstern, Julie.
  Organizing from the inside out for teens : the foolproof system for organizing your
  room, your time, and your life / Julie Morgenstern and Jessi Morgenstern-Colón.
      p. cm.
  Includes index.
  ISBN: 0-8050-6470-2 (pbk.)
    1. Teenagers—Life skills guides. 2. Time management. [1. Orderliness.]
  I. Morgenstern-Colón, Jessi. II. Title.
  HQ796 .M623 2002
  646.7'00835—dc21   2002068552

Henry Holt books are available for special promotions and premiums.
For details contact: Director, Special Markets.

First Owl Books Edition 2002

Designed by Debbie Glasserman

Printed in the United States of America
10 9 8 7 6 5 4 3

To teens everywhere,

in celebration of who you are,

and your capacity to make your dreams come true

CONTENTS

Jessi Says:
Why Get Organized?

So, you want to get organized. Well, there are a couple of things to get straight first.

You may have gotten this book from a parent, a teacher, a friend's sister's boyfriend's great-grandmother, or you may have bought it for yourself. It doesn't really matter where you got it, as long as you're reading it because you really, genuinely want to get organized. If you're planning to read this just to get people off your back, you can put the book down right now. Organizing is only worth the effort if you are motivated to do it for yourself; *you* have to want this.

And more than that: you should understand *why* you want it. Look, I'm a teenager, too. I know what it's like to have five hours of homework, extracurricular passions that you want to escape into every day after school, and an active social life. All this while constantly being told both to "Never stop adding to your college résumé!" and "Take advantage of your teen years. Use this time to discover yourself!" This book was written to help you set up a system that will enable you to do it all, or at least accomplish more within your given schedule and space.

Have you ever heard the saying "The shoemaker's children never have shoes"? Though I am the daughter of a professional organizer, I have not always been as organized as I am today. It was not some talent passed on through birth; I didn't even learn it at an early age. I have struggled with the issue for years, partly because I didn't feel the need to get organized for a long time, and also I thought being disorganized was the only way I could distinguish myself from my mom and let the world see that I was my own person.

To my mom's credit—although she tried to get my room into shape for years—she let me find my own way about it, all the while pointing out to me the ways in which I was already organized. I was never late for anything; my stuffed animals were always organized neatly by personality; my Barbies (all 102 of them) were in a big bin, which I bought for $5 at a flea market; and my books were all on a shelf in order grouped by type: picture books, easy readers, chapter books, poetry, and series books (*Minnie-n-Me*, *Babysitter's Club*, C. S. Lewis).

Yet, throughout elementary school, the rest of my room was always a total wreck. I'd lose game pieces, toys, and friends' phone numbers all the time. I'd often forget to do my homework, or was unable to find it in the piles of my room. Sometimes I'd even lose clothing–I can't tell you how many mornings I could come up with only one sneaker–or couldn't put my hands on my backpack. I thought that this was just the way things were and, as a result, never bothered to try to change.

It wasn't until I entered junior high school that I felt the need to do something about the chaos. At the time, school was not my top priority: dance and my social life came first. So I focused my organizing efforts on my areas of interest. I began by separating my dance clothes into a drawer and putting my dance shoes in boxes. I created a file for all my forms and dance information. To keep track of all my friends' phone numbers, I wrote each person's name and number on a color-coded Post-it, depending on where I'd first met them (junior high school, elementary school, dance school, or camp). I tacked these Post-its on the wall in four clusters. From then on, I could find any phone number at a glance and track how well I was balancing my time between my various social groups. And I always knew where my dance stuff was.

In high school, I began to understand the importance of doing well in classes and decided to get that part of my life under control as well. My schedule had begun to intensify, and I decided that if I wanted to do my best at school and still find time for the things I enjoyed the most, I'd have to quit worrying about being too much like my mom or what others thought.

I organized my school papers into a series of binders so that I'd always know what I needed and when. Then I created a matching filing system at home. At the end of each semester, I emptied the binders into the folders and started out fresh. This way I had a logical place for my work all year long. I also began using a planner and a schedule on my computer to carefully structure my days to make the most of them, planning time for my homework, my dance classes, and all my other activities. I got a shelf and drawers for my locker, so that instead of just throwing everything into a big pile, I could make better use of the space and locate anything I needed quickly.

Today, after years of staying organized, I am happy to report that I have succeeded in creating an effective system. But what's most important is that it's my *own* system—not one that my mother, or anyone else for that matter, tried to force on me. That's why it works. And that's what this book will do for you. It won't tell you how to run your life, where exactly to place each hook on the wall, or which classes to take to make your life easier. But it will help you figure out a way to turn over a new leaf and make the most of your space as well as your time.

I can't promise that you're going to get everything done and still get ten hours of sleep at night. What I can promise you, however, is that at the end of this process you'll be able to increase and make the most out of your free time. You'll be amazed how much time is gained when you don't have to search for your stuff, or when you know exactly what your plans are ahead of time. We all know that we're living in a crazy world that demands a lot from us. The organizing process is very grounding. It's a great way to gain control of your life and world.

Getting organized does not mean becoming neat or cleaning up. You may be looking around your room right now and seeing something that looks like a disaster area, and yet you may still be perfectly on top of things. In Chapter 1, you'll find a self-assessment that will help you figure out if you are in fact already organized. Organizing is not about how things look; it's about knowing where your stuff is, keeping your schedule together, and making your space and time work for you.

We're all organized in one way or another, whether we know it or not. It may be something as seemingly insignificant as the way you get your math homework done or how you arrange your books. But if it works for you, that's a start. The next step is figuring out what makes your organized areas so effective and applying that approach to the less organized parts of your life. Don't think that you'll never be able to pull it all together. Anyone can be organized; it's *not* an inborn talent. It's a skill that can be learned.

This book is divided into three main parts: "The Basics," "Organizing Your Space," and "Organizing Your Time." Start by reading "The Basics" (the first two chapters of the book). They'll give you the foundation you need to make all your future efforts a success. Then skip around to the specific chapters in Parts 2 and 3 that you're most interested in, to speed up your efforts to get organized from the inside out.

So, now that you're sure you're doing this for yourself, and you know why, let's get going.

PART 1

The Basics

What's Holding You Back?

If you're reading this book, chances are that you think you are a disorganized person (or someone you know thinks you are). You've been sometimes lovingly, and other times scoldingly, referred to as a slob, mess-aholic, or pack rat.

We're going to bust a lot of myths about getting organized, and here is the first one. *Organizing is not about discipline. It's about design.* If your system is a custom fit for you, maintaining it will be a breeze. You don't have to change who you are to get organized. You have to work *with* your natural habits and goals. You design the system to support you, not to change you.

Myth: Organizing is the same as being neat.
Fact: Organizing is *not* about how a space looks, but how it functions.

In the game of organization, substance is what matters, not style. Many people keep their rooms looking so neat and clean, you'd think you could eat off their floor. However, when push comes to shove, they can never find anything—because inside their drawers and closets, it's utter chaos. Others have rooms that are all piles, a stack of papers here, a mountain of clothes there, but when it's time to look for something they need, they can find it within seconds.

Messy does not equal disorganized. It doesn't matter if people think that your room looks like a disaster area. Here's the definition of organizing this book is based on: If you know where your stuff is, are able to find what you need when you need it, and are comfortable in your space, then you're organized! If you're happy with your schedule and comfortable with where your time is spent, then you are a good time manager. In that case you probably don't even need to read any further. But be honest with yourself. Take the following self-assessment to see if your piles are a help or a hindrance and if you're really as organized as you'd like to be.

DO YOU NEED THIS BOOK?

Take this assessment to determine if you are as organized as you'd like to be:

1.	True	False	I can find anything I need in two minutes or less.
2.	T	F	I feel in control of my space, time, and papers.
3.	T	F	Cleanup is quick because I know where everything goes.
4.	T	F	I am rarely late.
5.	T	F	I hardly ever lose things.
6.	T	F	Getting ready to go out is a smooth process.
7.	T	F	Procrastination is rarely a problem for me.
8.	T	F	I get my homework done on time and am pleased with the results.
9.	T	F	I feel happy with what I accomplish every day.
10.	T	F	I rarely hear myself apologizing for how my room looks.
11.	T	F	I am comfortable in my space.
12.	T	F	I don't think being disorganized is an obstacle to my success.

If you answered "false" to three or more of the above questions, keep reading. This book was written expressly for you. It will teach you how to organize your life so that you can succeed in all your goals and still find enough time to enjoy yourself.

Myth: Organizing is a talent you're either born with or not.
Fact: Organizing is a learnable *skill*.

You've tried to get organized in the past. Many times. Well, at least you've thought about it. You've spent marathon weekends sorting through the clutter in your room, getting rid of as much as you can, yet within days you're right back to the way it looked before. Your parents have doled out big bucks for every kind of calendar, Palm Pilot, and pager ever invented, alarm clocks that sing your favorite show tunes . . . but you still find yourself racing behind the clock.

You're envious of the kids who seem to have it all together, who fit in a million after-school activities, get straight A's, are never late for anything, and always know where their keys are.

Is organizing a mysterious talent some lucky people are born with, while the rest of the world's poor, unfortunate souls (like you) are left to suffer? The truth is that organizing is a remarkably simple skill that anyone can learn. We have both learned it. And you can, too. That's what this book is all about.

Say it out loud: I am *not* a disorganized person! The fact is, everybody is organized somewhere. No matter how messy your room is, no matter how often you have lost your library books or scrambled at the last minute to do your homework, there's no doubt that somewhere—buried under the piles, hidden inside the chaos—there are some systems that are working for you. Right now, before reading any further, take a moment to define where you *are* organized by consulting the "Where Are *You* Organized?" assessment on the following page. Why start there, you ask? Because it builds confidence. It gives you energy. And it's the truth.

WHERE ARE *YOU* ORGANIZED?

Everybody is organized in some parts of his or her life, disorganized in others. Start this process on a positive note by identifying the areas in which you are organized: is it your homework, clothes, bedroom, memorabilia, collections, social life, time, photos, sock drawer? Then move on to the areas that need improvement. Examples:

Lilly Y., 17, Georgia

What's organized: My clothes and social life
What's not: My school stuff and studying

Jonathan S., 15, New York

What's organized: My homework
What's not: My bedroom and sports gear

Ariela N., 16, Florida

What's organized: My photos and memorabilia
What's not: My papers and school supplies

Your turn:

What's organized: _____
What's not: _____

Myth: Organizing is about throwing things away.
Fact: You can keep everything that you want and still get organized.

"Look at all this junk!" "I gotta get rid of this clutter!" "I've got way too much stuff!" Many of us believe that organizing is about getting rid of as much "junk" as we possibly can. But organizing is *never* about throwing things away. It's about discovering what's important and giving yourself access to it. So instead of looking at organizing as a punishing process, like being stripped of all your treasures and gold, think of it as identifying what's important to you and honoring it by giving it a place in your space or your schedule.

Many of us are collectors at heart. Fortunately, organizing doesn't mean saying good-bye to all our treasures. You don't have to live like a monk to be organized. Instead, celebrate all your worldly possessions by arranging them in one place. For instance, you can keep your vast collection of concert T-shirts folded on one or two easy-to-reach shelves rather than leaving them strewn about your closet and stuffed in random drawers. Or, consolidate your zillions of photos into a matching set of boxes and albums so you can actually enjoy looking at them. After all, what's the point of gathering all of those wonderful treasures if you can't find them when you want them?

You may be wondering: If organizing is a skill that anyone can learn, why am I so disorganized? Most people believe that clutter is caused by laziness, sloppiness, or pure incompetence. That could be the biggest myth of all. All messes are not created equal. There are actually more causes for clutter than you can imagine, and none of them have to do with your being lazy (even if you are sometimes!).

Rather than beating yourself up and dismissing yourself as a hopeless case, take a look at the ten most common causes of disorganization described below. The good news is that every problem has a cure. By pinpointing the real reasons for your chaos, you'll take the first steps toward solving the problem and save yourself lots of time and energy in the process. Read through the following symptoms and see if you can get to the root of your clutter.

Organizational Roadblocks

SYMPTOMS

- ❐ I never put things back in the same place twice.
- ❐ I have new clothes, games, papers, or books and can't figure out where to put them.
- ❐ There are so many things I want to do, but I have no idea *when* to do them.

DIAGNOSIS: HOMELESS ITEMS AND TASKS

The bottom line is, you can't put something away if there's no place to put it. And you won't be able to plan a friend's party or finish your chemistry lab work if you haven't set aside time in your schedule to do it. If your room is overrun by piles and clutter, one reason may be that you have not designated homes for many of your things. As a dynamic and changing person, you probably acquire new possessions on a daily basis: every new year brings new interests and the accessories that go with it; every new class involves a new set of books. Your to-do list grows right alongside your expanding commitments. You end up with so much stuff to do and track, you get to the point that you don't know where to put anything anymore. So, you drop things anywhere, tuck tasks into any available pocket of space, and end up not getting to a lot of things.

 PRESCRIPTION

Create one single, permanent home for each item (or category of items) that you own. For example, pens, pencils, and markers could go in the top desk drawer; calculators, compasses, and rulers in the middle; spare paper and stationery in the bottom, permanently. That way, if you are in the middle of math homework, you know exactly which drawer to look in for your graphing calculator. It's actually not so complicated to designate a home for every item. Chapter 2 will give you a memorable and clever way to figure out what goes where so you'll never forget.

This rule also applies to your to-dos. You need to assign a specific home (or time) to each task on your to-do list. Pick the particular day and the time you will do various projects and take care of responsibilities—being specific will ensure they won't be forgotten. Part 3 of this book will teach you more about finding the best times to do various tasks and how to keep track of your plans.

SYMPTOMS

- ❏ I can't reach places where things belong.
- ❏ My doors, cabinets, and/or drawers are stuck.
- ❏ My bins are piled too high.
- ❏ I find that it becomes too hard to put things away.

DIAGNOSIS: INCONVEN-IENT STORAGE

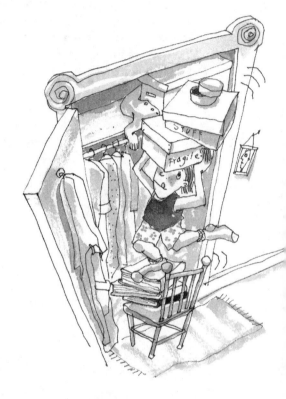

More than half the time, you *have* designated a home for your belongings, but those homes are just too hard to get to. The shelves are too high to reach. The dresser drawer is broken and too hard to open. The closet door is blocked by a big chair, which you have to shove out of the way just to hang up your clothes. The hamper is down the hall in the bathroom. No wonder your dirty clothes are piled on the floor of your room!

📝 PRESCRIPTION

Nobody will put things away if it's too hard. You've got to make the process more convenient. The secret is to store things where you use them, not necessarily where they fit. And fix or remove broken doors and drawers. This entire book is full of tips and suggestions for relocating items within arm's reach of where you use them.

✍ Julie's Work Journal:

Amy's Story

Amy, who is five feet two inches tall, was looking for a place in her room to store her board games. Many of the boxes were big and chunky and some were long and flat, and she decided that storing them on the long top shelf of her closet (seven feet off the ground) would be a good idea. Seemed logical at the time. But unbeknownst to Amy, this location was destined to cause problems.

Every time she wanted to put a game back where it belonged, she had to drag the desk chair to the closet and risk life and limb trying to keep her balance while plumbing the farthest reaches of the shelf. This system didn't hold up for long, and pretty soon she (and her friends) were tripping over game pieces scattered all over the floor. We moved her games to an underbed drawer on wheels. That placed her games right next to where they were used. Easy access, easy cleanup.

SYMPTOMS

- ❏ My filing system is way too confusing to me.
- ❏ I have boxes inside boxes inside drawers on my shelves.
- ❏ I tried organizing my CDs with number codes, but I can't remember what the codes mean.
- ❏ I have too many drawers and cubbies to remember what goes where.

DIAGNOSIS: OVERLY COMPLEX SYSTEM

An overly complex system becomes a black hole—things go in but they never come out. Trust in your system disintegrates faster than a sumo wrestler in quicksand, and you stop putting things away because you're afraid you'll never see them again.

Erez was working on a community service project that he was really excited about, but keeping track of all the paperwork was a huge challenge. There were flyers and announcements for volunteers; letters to the city to ask for special permissions; plans and invitations for fund-raising events; phone numbers and e-mail addresses for all the volunteers; multiple copies of meeting notes. He created a new folder for every separate piece of paper he acquired, and pretty soon he never knew where to look. His filing system got so complicated, he stopped using it, and all the papers ended up in a big pile on the floor next to his desk.

When it comes to time management, disorganization can result when you take an overly complex approach to certain large projects. Ariele had an oral history project to do. Although she was only required to interview three people, she decided to interview ten. In preparation for each interview, she also decided she needed to read five or six history books. Once she finished interviewing so many people, it would take her months to weed through and interpret all her data. She had unnecessarily overcomplicated it.

 PRESCRIPTION

The solution here is to simplify your system. When it comes to stuff, always look for the broadest categories to sort your belongings into. When it comes to overwhelming projects, you need to learn how to break them down into small, manageable steps. The kindergarten model in Chapter 2 will help you simplify both organizing and time-management systems so that there's only one logical place to put or find any item. Part 3 on time management will give you lots of specific examples of breaking tasks down into smaller parts.

SYMPTOMS

- ❐ All of my drawers, closets, and shelves are filled to capacity.
- ❐ My containers are bulging with overflowing contents.
- ❐ My to-do list goes on for six pages. I have way too much to do, but not enough time.
- ❐ No matter how busy I am, there's still so much more to do.

DIAGNOSIS: MORE STUFF THAN SPACE

If your dresser is buckling under the pressure of crammed drawers, your closet is packed to capacity, and even your windowsill hasn't seen the light of day in years, you may be suffering from a clear-cut case of object overload. This can happen in a little room or a big room but the feeling is that your stuff is squeezing *you* out. If your to-do list never stops and you barely have time to eat, you may also be suffering from an unrealistic workload. We don't need to tell you: a teen's life can be very hectic and demanding. Things may have been pretty calm and manageable in elementary school, but once you hit junior high school, BLAM, the pressure started to pile on. Too much work, too much responsibility, and too many expectations.

PRESCRIPTION

There are two main ways to tackle this situation:

1. Reduce the amount of stuff/activities.
2. Maximize the amount of storage/time in your day.

Getting rid of things can be one of the hardest parts of organizing, but there are ways to make it easier if it's really necessary to make sure you still have room for your bed! No matter how large or small your space is, making a little space go a long way is one of the crucial organizational skills this book will help you acquire.

In every chapter, you'll learn how to sort through your items and decide what to keep and what to toss. You'll also discover new ways of stretching space and finding storage where none seems to exist.

On the time front: When your workload gets too heavy, you need to learn how to say no, how to delay certain tasks and maximize your energy and time every day. Part 3 of this book is entirely devoted to giving you the time-management skills needed to find the right balance, eliminate procrastination, and work with your natural rhythms and preferences to get the most out of each day. You may actually have enough time on your hands, but simply need to use it better.

SYMPTOMS

☐ I'm afraid if I put anything away, I'll never find it again.
☐ If I can't see things, I forget I own them.
☐ I leave things out to remember to do them, but forget they are there.

DIAGNOSIS: THE "OUT OF SIGHT, OUT OF MIND!" MIND-SET

Many of us are afraid that if we put things away in a closet or a drawer we will forget they exist. So we leave things out to remember them, a visual to-do list. For example, you stack the overdue library books by your door so that you'll remember to grab them before you leave for school. On your dresser, you may have a pair of jeans that need mending, a sweater that you have to return to your friend who left it at your house last time she slept over, and a permission slip that you have to get your mom to sign. Visual reminders are great if they actually work. However, for most people, leaving everything out in the open makes their sight go blurry. Piles blend into one another, making visual reminders virtually invisible, and you begin to ignore them.

PRESCRIPTION

If the piles are not doing their job to keep you on track, the solution is to find a new, more effective reminder system. This usually involves combining a simple storage system so your stuff is always in the same, reliable place, along with a to-do list, planner, or calendar to tell you what you need to do. The kindergarten model in Chapter 2 offers a foolproof way of organizing spaces so you never lose or forget what you own. Chapter 7 will teach you how to select and use a to-do list, planner, or agenda to remind you what you need to do and when you need to do it.

SYMPTOMS

- ❑ I share a room with a disorganized sibling.
- ❑ My stuff keeps getting taken by my sister/brother.
- ❑ I want to move to the attic—any space that's just mine.
- ❑ Everyone in my family is a pack rat.
- ❑ My house is too cluttered to bring friends home.
- ❑ Every time I set aside an hour to tackle one of my to-dos, my parents ask me to do something else.

DIAGNOSIS: DISORGANIZED FAMILY

In your quest for a sane, peaceful, and organized environment, living with a disorganized family can be one of the most difficult hurdles to clear. There's nothing more frustrating than trying to establish order in a room you share with a sib who is only too happy to live out the rest of his or her days in a pigsty. It's equally frustrating when you have your supplies really well organized, and family members keep borrowing them without returning them because they can never find their own. In a chaotically run household, everything often happens at the last minute, making it very hard for you to make and stick to any plans of your own. If everyone in your family—from your grandfather on down to your parents, aunts, and uncles—is disorganized, carving out your own little oasis of order can present a major challenge.

 PRESCRIPTION

Aspiring to neatness in a disorganized family can be like trying to lose weight in an overweight family—there can be lots of guilt and anger on both sides. Recognize that organizing can start with just *your* space. In fact, if your family seems disinterested in getting organized, give up trying to motivate them to see things your way and focus exclusively on your own individual area. Let everybody know that you're not trying to convert them. You just want your space to be organized.

If you are sharing a room, try subdividing the space in a way that gives each of you your individual sections. Screens, beads, and furniture can all work well as room dividers. Label your supplies with a label maker—and start charging your sib a lending fee every time he or she has borrowed things without returning them. Also, give special consideration to who's in the front half of the room and who's in the back. If you can't stand looking at the clutter, think about taking the half of the room closest to the door. If you prefer the privacy, you can go in the back and let your sibling have the front so that your sib doesn't have to walk through your space to get to his or hers.

SYMPTOMS

❏ I am fearful that getting organized will squelch my creativity.
❏ I love spontaneity and unpredictability.
❏ I find structure too confining.
❏ Part of my charm lies in the fact that I am disorganized.

DIAGNOSIS: FEAR OF LOSING INDIVIDUALITY

Perhaps being disorganized is your fun and kooky trademark. You can often be heard complaining about how scattered and disorganized you are, but deep inside you're kind of proud of your charming and offbeat lifestyle. Maybe you're even afraid that getting organized will transform you from a free spirit into a tense obsessive-compulsive type . . . your creativity will disappear, you won't be as dramatic or as interesting, people won't like you as much, and then where will you be?

 **PRESCRIPTION**

Relax. An organizational system does not mean taking leave of your personality. As you'll see in the chapters to come, a good system can both reflect and encourage your creative, dramatic, and impulsive side by being just as creative and visually stimulating as you are. If you've never tried organizing, it takes a leap of faith to discover that you'll find even more time for your creative projects if you're organized. Just think of how many ideas you never get to pursue because you can't find the tools or the time you need. The fact is that you're a creative person and your brain is going to keep generating all these ideas. The question is, are you going to be organized enough to take them on?

SYMPTOMS

- ❐ I can't stand the repetitiveness of putting things away.
- ❐ I jump from one exciting project to the next without taking time to clean up.

❐ Cleaning up feels like a complete waste of time that could be spent having fun.

❐ Entering info into my Palm Pilot is so dull I never end up doing it.

DIAGNOSIS: BELIEF THAT ORGANIZING IS BORING

OK–let's face it. "Tidying up" can seem about as exciting as watching paint dry. And sometimes, if something's not fun, it's awfully hard to motivate yourself to do it. So, what can you do to combat this resistance based on boredom?

 PRESCRIPTION

First of all, don't try to convince yourself that cleanup is fun and exciting. But instead of concentrating on how boring the process is, think about how great it feels to find things when you're looking for them. So you're really not putting things away; you're just preparing them for the next time you need them. Or consider how calming and grounding it can be to find time for all your activities. When life is really chaotic, organizing your time and schedule can be a welcome break from the chaos and a very soothing experience. You can also find motivation in self-bribery. Promise yourself that as soon as you put everything away or stick to a schedule, you can call a friend, curl up with a book, have your favorite snack, watch your favorite show, take your dog for a run. In Chapters 4, 5, and 6, you'll find techniques for designing your space so that it takes only three to five minutes to clean it up–no matter how messy it gets. So if you have a favorite TV show, straighten up for five minutes before it starts and then watch the show as a reward for a job well done. Once this becomes routine, you'll be surprised how easily it sticks.

SYMPTOMS

❏ I can't bear to throw anything out.
❏ I am emotionally attached to every object I've ever owned.
❏ I feel like I am throwing out part of myself when I get rid of things.
❏ I can't imagine giving up my art class. I've been taking it with my best friend since I was six.

DIAGNOSIS: SENTIMENTAL ATTACHMENT

Often, it's hard to let go of things we aren't using anymore because we infuse them with a tremendous amount of meaning. It becomes harder still if you add feelings to your inanimate objects. You're ready to throw away the bunny, but you're afraid his feelings will be hurt.

Hanging on to some symbols of your past is important. But it's all a matter of quantity. If you are saving so much from your past that there is no room for the new, it's time to reconsider just how much you are saving. In times like these, it's important to remember that our identity comes from within, not from what we own.

 PRESCRIPTION

Give yourself permission to let things go. Your interests and hobbies are changing all the time. Because teen years are a time of such tremendous and constant change, once a year take a day to look around your room and figure out what no longer fits in. Review your schedule and see which activities you're holding on to for purely sentimental reasons. None of this is to say that *all* of your old stuff needs to go. Keep a few symbols from each important time in your past and throw away the rest. Chapter 6 will help you select and organize your memorabilia so that you can actually enjoy it while still making room for new things in your life. This way, you get to save some of the stuff that reminds you who you were, but you still have room for the new expressions of yourself.

Jessi Says

Getting Beyond the Boredom

When I was eight years old I had an eye-opening experience that gave me the hope that I could actually get my room into shape. As a professional organizer, my mom had organized my room numerous times—everything had a place (one of the cardinal rules of organizing). But my room would still become messy, because I didn't put anything away. This, of course, was as frustrating for her as it was for me. It so happened that she was giving an organizing workshop on National Take Your Daughters to Work Day, and I decided to attend. I never could have predicted the outcome.

In teaching the class, my mom focused on how important it was to design your system based on the way you think, taking into account your natural habits and needs. I decided that not all hope was lost. On the way home from the workshop, I told my mom that we just hadn't found the right system for me yet.

"Do you want my help?" Yes was the answer. "Let's set up an appointment." We agreed to meet the following evening.

During the consultation, I was treated as a client. My mom asked me what I needed places for and where I thought those items should be placed. As I scanned the room, I realized it was in fact already set up pretty well. Then came her next question: "If everything is where it should be and it's grouped the way you think, what do you think the problem is?"

"I guess I just don't like to put things away," I evaluated. "Is it OK with you if you don't put things away?" "No, I can't use my room." "So, if you don't like putting things away, can you think of something you do enjoy doing?" I responded, "I like going on-line."

Her suggestion was to set up a reward system. I was offered a coupon for fifteen minutes of AOL time for every day I cleaned my room. I asked, "Can I save them up so that I can have a twenty-four-hour marathon?" She said yes.

This system really worked. The key was that it was *my* goal and *my* reward system. We used this system for a couple of months. Then I got used to cleaning up automatically and started to enjoy the fact that I could find things. The reward system was a bridge to a new set of habits.

SYMPTOMS

- ❐ I don't know how to choose what's important and what's not.
- ❐ It's hard for me to prioritize.
- ❐ I feel interested in so many things—I'm overwhelmed.
- ❐ I'm not sure in what direction my life is going.

DIAGNOSIS: UNCLEAR GOALS AND PRIORITIES

Obviously, if you know what your goals are, figuring out what belongings you need and how to spend your time to accomplish them will be much easier. However, as a teenager you may not yet know what you want to accomplish in your life. One day you're playing guitar and hoping to be the next Jimi Hendrix; the next day you're thinking about inventing a better computer and giving Bill Gates a run for his billions.

 PRESCRIPTION

Even if your interests aren't set in stone, it doesn't mean that you can't be organized. While you're trying to decide what you're going to do with the rest of your life, you should organize your time and space to reflect who you are right now. Ask yourself: What's important to me now?

If you can't think of any good answers, think about how you spend your days. What brings you the most happiness, gives you a sense of accomplishment, and generally makes life enjoyable? Answering these questions will give you a good idea of what your interests are today.

Sometimes we have a hard time admitting what's important. We may secretly know the answer but feel shy or insecure about our desires. We aren't sure if it's OK to want these things. It may be different from what our parents, friends, teachers, and relatives want. The formula in this book is based on giving yourself permission to be who you are and designing a system to fit your current ideas about life—not the ideas you had two years ago or the ideas you think you "should" have.

Organizing from the inside out is a way to dig deep down into yourself, learn about who you really are, and build your confidence in a sometimes overwhelming world. The entire process is built around finding and expressing your unique gifts. Ultimately, it frees you to be your best self and can help boost your self-confidence.

Now that we've busted a lot of the organizing myths and figured out what's been holding you back, it's time to start getting organized! Let's get going!

2

Three Steps to Success: Inside-Out Organizing

You are a unique individual, still discovering who you are and finding ways to express that. *Organizing from the inside out* taps into your individuality, helping you learn to organize your time, space, and belongings in a way that makes sense to you. For instance, one person might organize her CDs alphabetically by artist, another by type of music, and a third chronologically by date of purchase. One person may do his or her best work in the morning, another at night. In the end, it doesn't matter how you choose to organize yourself; if your system works for you, that's what counts.

Organizing from the inside out guides you in building a custom-made system that works because it reflects what's important to you and gives you access to it. It is a process that helps you discover and applaud who you are and what you want instead of forcing you to conform to some one-size-supposedly-fits-all program. The final result is an organizational system that makes you feel good about yourself, helps you accomplish all of your goals, and is natural and easy to maintain.

How do you know if you are making the mistake of organizing yourself from the *outside in*? If you are copying someone else's system even though it doesn't work for you, if you are spending a fortune on baskets, bins, planners, and sorters at every Home Depot you encounter, or if you are trying to drum organizing "rules" into your head when they just don't make sense to you, it's time to rethink your strategy. Organizing from the outside in doesn't work because it doesn't take into account your distinctive personality, natural habits, or way of thinking. Results are usually short-term, because they are not a natural fit.

THREE STEPS TO SUCCESS

No matter how long the clutter has been building up, how huge the piles, or how crammed your daily planner, there are three simple, reliable steps that will put you back in control. Whether you are organizing your clothes, room, or schedule, these three steps will lead you to solutions that will fit your unique needs, goals, and style.

Remember, there is no one perfect organizing system that will work for everyone. The three steps of organizing from the inside out are simply a *process* to help you find the organizing solution that is a custom fit for you. The three steps are:

- Analyze
    - Strategize
        - Attack

✎ Julie's Work Journal:

Pamela's Story

Pamela, a fun-loving sixteen-year-old, loves to shop and is a great bargain hunter. Her bedroom was packed to the brim with what seemed like thousands of treasures. Some items were purely practical—tons of clothes, books, school supplies. Some were just for fun—her hamster along with its cage and food, a new kind of light-up Frisbee, special dual-headsets she bought to share with a friend for a class trip. There was lots of memorabilia—stuffed animals, toys from her childhood, many boxes of photos and souvenirs from everywhere she went. Her best friend described her as a snowball—"Pamela just rolls around and accumulates stuff." She bought every kind of little device invented—mini scissors, mini sewing kit, snacks in noncrushable containers for her travels. She loved feeling prepared for anything. The only problem was . . . she often couldn't find the things she'd bought when she needed them.

Periodically—during a school vacation or on a long weekend—she'd tackle the job of organizing her room. Every time, she'd focus on trying to get rid of stuff. She did that because her friends and family always told her she was a pack rat and that throwing things away was the only way she'd ever get organized. But she never got very far.

Digging through the piles, she'd unearth all kinds of long-forgotten trinkets with a thrill. Exclamations of "Wow, I forgot I had this!" "Oh, I've been looking for that!" and "No WAY can I get rid of this!" would grind her mission to a halt. Getting rid of anything was torture for her. And the truth is, it wasn't necessary.

Pamela was trying to organize herself from the outside in. She had the kind of personality that loved to own lots of sentimental and useful things—focusing on getting rid of things went completely against her nature. And so it didn't work. Pamela's real problem was not that she had too much stuff. Her only frustration was that she couldn't *find* things when she needed them. So, the task was not to get rid of things—it was simply to better organize what she had.

As we looked around her room, we discovered that her clothes were incredibly organized. Inside her closet, her huge wardrobe was arranged neatly on her shelves in groupings—short sleeve, long sleeve, spaghetti straps; jeans, capris, corduroys, etc. She could always locate exactly the shirt, skirt, or pair of pants she wanted.

All Pamela had to do was apply the same approach to the other categories of her stuff. And that's what she did. We grouped similar items and designated one whole section in her room for all of her memorabilia, another area for school stuff, two shelves for games, and one cabinet for practical gadgets and useful objects. Suddenly, Pamela could get her hands on anything she wanted at any time. She never lost another textbook or miniature fan again. By organizing from the inside out, Pamela had achieved her unique goal.

This chapter will help you understand the basics of what to do and how each step will get you to the end no matter which area of your life needs organizing. Future chapters will follow this format, so it's important to read this chapter before jumping ahead. Now, let's get started!

STEP 1: ANALYZE

The biggest challenge to getting organized is knowing where to start. Most people approach the organizing process backward. They begin by diving into the clutter, getting rid of things, or searching for shortcuts and quick solutions to their scheduling problems. Untangling a big jumble of clutter can be overwhelming. There are a lot of decisions to make.

In order to make the right decisions for you, you need to step back from the chaos and think things through a little. It's critical to assess your current situation so you can tune in to your specific needs and preferences. No matter what you are organizing—from your book bag to your overloaded schedule—begin by asking yourself the following four key questions:

1. What's working and what's not?
2. What's your Essential 7?
3. What's the payoff?
4. What's the problem?

These four "analyze" questions will help you scope out the terrain before you begin your journey. They transform your approach from the general and useless ("Everything is a complete mess!") to the specific and practical ("I can never find my schoolbooks in the morning when I need to leave for school"). And they keep you motivated and focused.

Keep in mind that you must answer the same four questions before you begin *any* organizing project. Whether you're trying to tidy up your bedroom, your locker, your study habits, or your social life, you'll find that stepping back to assess the situation first will tell you everything you need to know to custom-design your system.

It takes only a few minutes to answer these questions, but this time will be the best investment you'll ever make, saving you hours of frustration, freeing you up to focus your efforts only where they're needed, and ensuring that your design is a perfect fit.

Be sure to write out your answers. Seeing them in black and white will help clarify your thinking. As you read through this chapter, answer these questions in general terms, addressing the big picture of all organizing challenges ahead of you (e.g., time, space, closets, social life). Later, when you turn to the chapters that target problem areas, you will answer the questions again, this time tailored to the specific area you are trying to organize.

By the end of this chapter, you'll be ready to create a plan of action and prioritize the projects you'll need to tackle in the process.

Question #1: What's Working and What's Not?

Always begin your organizing assessment by asking yourself what already works well for you and what isn't working at all. Let's start with what is working first.

What's Working?

Buried inside every mess are a few effective organizing systems. Look closely. Think hard. What little systems do you have that work and are stress-free? Which areas of your life seem to be going better than others? What objects can you always count on finding? Maybe it's the dresser drawer that holds all your running clothes or the CD case in your backpack. Maybe you are better at organizing your time than your space.

There are a great deal of advantages to identifying and preserving what's working. First, you'll save time and energy. You don't need to reorganize anything that works for you. As the saying goes: If it ain't broke, don't fix it. Second, the presence of an orderly area in your otherwise cluttered universe serves as a confidence booster. The fact is, if you can organize one thing, you can organize anything. And last but not least, figuring out what's working helps you understand your individual organizing preferences. By studying the systems that work—and asking yourself why—you will learn what appeals to you, so you can then replicate those solutions in other, less together areas of your life.

👍 What's Working?

Complete the following sentences (feel free to write down as many responses as come to mind):

1. I can always find my _____
   _____

2. I always have a place to put my _____
   _____

3. I like the current setup of my _____
   _____

4. No matter how busy I get, I always find time for _____
   _____

5. My goals are well defined when it comes to_____
   _____

Possible responses to the above fill-in-the-blanks could be:
1. I can always find my <u>clothes, books, keys, baseball glove, CDs and DVDs, clean socks.</u>
2. I always have a place to put my <u>magazines, water glass at night, cellphone charger, glasses/contacts, tennis racket, school supplies.</u>
3. I like the current setup of my <u>dresser drawers, study schedule, address book, jewelry box, shoe rack.</u>
4. No matter how busy I get, I always find time for <u>sewing, my friends, playing the piano, church, soccer practice, dinner with my family.</u>
5. My goals are well defined when it comes to <u>school, my social life, family life, career, religion.</u>

Now, look at your list. Ask yourself what it is about the above systems that works for you. Is it a matter of convenience, simplicity, location, size? Perhaps your address book is organized alphabetically by first name. Maybe you could mirror that system in your CD collection. Maybe your notebooks are color coded. Perhaps you could create a matching color-coded filing system. Maybe you work through your homework class by class. You could apply that sense of order to your chores, tackling them room by room. The point is that these systems reveal hints about what you like, what appeals to you, and where your organizing strengths lie.

What's Not Working?

Now that you've identified what works, it's time to identify everything that needs fixing. This is one of those rare moments in life when you get the opportunity to whine as freely as you like.

As you answer the following questions, keep in mind that this is *not* about what's not working for your parents, your friends, your relatives, your teachers, your guidance counselors, and your neighbor's cocker spaniel. It's about what's not working for *you*. If the whole world thinks you're disorganized, but you know exactly where everything is and never miss a meeting or class, then you're golden. If there are any parts of your space or your life where you are not performing to your best ability, then that's what you need to focus on. Don't judge, just write.

👎 What's Not Working?

Complete the following statements. If you come up with more than one response to each (and you probably will), be sure to write them all down.

1. I can never find my _____
   _____

2. I have no place to put my _____
   _____

3. I don't have enough time for _____
   _____

4. I procrastinate whenever I have to _____
_____

5. I have a hard time finishing _____
_____

Possible responses to the above questions could be:
1. I can never find my <u>keys, watch, glasses, wallet, calculator, gloves.</u>
2. I have no place to put my <u>sneakers, sleeping bag, stapler, photos, retainer, library books, videotapes.</u>
3. I don't have enough time for <u>sleeping, my friends, just relaxing, completing my homework, extracurricular activities.</u>
4. I procrastinate whenever I have to <u>do a research project, read a book for school, take out the trash, walk the dog, pack for a trip, go to bed.</u>
5. I have a hard time finishing <u>my chores, homework, piano practice, assembling my photo albums, math problems.</u>

If you are having a hard time coming up with a thorough list of what's not working, keep a "problems log" for a week. Write down everything that annoys you in a designated notepad each day, and you'll have a complete list by week's end.

Brainstorm in the actual space you plan to organize. Responses will come to you more easily because reminders of the problems will be staring you in the face.

Question #2: What's Your Essential 7?

Ideally, our spaces and schedules would be filled only with things we use, love, and care about. This would make finding and putting things away so much easier, and it would make us feel good about every task and to-do on our schedules. However, we often hang on to things that *used* to be important to us or things we thought would be important to us *someday* (but they turn out not to be).

We promised earlier that organizing from the inside out focuses not on *getting rid of things* but on *identifying what is important to you* and giving you easy access to those items. The Essential 7 question helps you zero in on what really counts.

Before diving into the mess of your room, locker, or complicated to-do list, name the seven most important items in the area you are about to organize. What are the objects you are constantly looking for and need most often? What are the activities you do that are the most meaningful and/or useful to you?

Asking this question before you get lost in the chaos tells you a lot about who you are right now and will serve as a firm foundation for any system you design. It will make the sorting and tossing process that comes later on much easier. It will keep you focused and you'll be able to deal calmly and rationally with the many tempting "finds" you come across during your archaeological dig.

Voices from Teens

Each teen's Essential 7 list reveals a lot about his or her personality and will vary as widely as the individuals making the lists. Here are some examples of how different one teen's list can be from the next.

My Bedroom—The Essential 7

Sean P., 12, Michigan
1. Stereo
2. Playstation
3. String bass
4. Bible
5. Cat
6. Computer
7. Bear

Serena M., 16, New York
1. Sketchbook
2. Colored pencils
3. *New Yorker* magazine covers
4. Sheet music
5. CD player
6. Books
7. Roller blades

My Locker—The Essential 7

Josiane L., 14, Massachusetts
1. Bio book
2. My calculators (graphic and scientific)
3. Pencil case
4. Algebra and trig book
5. Agenda
6. Notebooks
7. Body mists

Tiffany G., 16, New Orleans
1. Worksheets for class
2. Junior steering committee papers
3. Books
4. Notes for music (choir class)
5. Calendar
6. Money
7. Cell phone

My Schedule—The Essential 7

Sarah S., 15, Ohio
1. Homework
2. Drama
3. Scrapbooking
4. Family time
5. Youth group
6. Friends
7. Reading

Eric S., 17, New York
1. Robot building
2. Homework
3. College search
4. Job
5. TV
6. Internet
7. Chess team

% Pareto's 80/20 Rule

Have you ever heard of the Pareto's 80/20 Rule? It's a phenomenon that can be applied to many things, but it applies to organizing in the following way. Most people don't use about 80 percent of what they own. They wear the same 20 percent of clothes over and over, listen to the same 20 percent of their CD collection, watch the same 20 percent of their videos. The Essential 7 question helps you find your 20 percent.

Having trouble zeroing in on what's important to you? Name seven things that you would take with you if there was a fire in your house.

Write down everything you need to do on one master to-do list. Look the list over and pick seven things that would give you the biggest sense of accomplishment if you got them done.

Question #3: What's the Payoff?

No matter how you slice it, organizing takes time, effort, and lots of concentration. In the middle of any organizing project, it's easy to get tired, become distracted, or lose interest. To prevent that from stopping you in your tracks, it helps to articulate and write down what's driving you at the peak of your motivation.

What is the actual point of getting organized? What do you really want to accomplish? Usually it's something beyond the clutter that is motivating you. You are seeking some reward that goes beyond a tidy room or neatly arranged to-do list.

Here are some of the payoffs identified by other teens:

💬 "I want to be able to add volunteering to my already full schedule, without having anything else suffer."
—Janine L., 17, New Jersey

💬 "I want to improve my reputation in my school so I can join the peer leadership team next year."
—Jared S., 13, Wyoming

💬 "I miss spending time with my friends. I have no social life anymore because my time is so out of control."
—Casey P., 16, Ohio

💬 "I want to be able to spend more time with my little sister. She's going through a rough time and I think I could help her."
—Nour S., 17, New York

💬 "I'm always freaking out because I can't find anything in my room. I want to reduce the stress in my life!"
—Liz V., 15, New York

💬 "I want my parents to give me more freedom—but I have to prove to them that I can be more responsible and not forget stuff."
—Bela K., 14, Florida

🖎 Julie's Work Journal:

Jack's Story

Jack was a very smart, supercreative fifteen-year-old. He played the piano, painted watercolors, went to poetry slams, and rode his skateboard a lot. He didn't collect too much stuff, and most of what he did have was pretty well organized. His CDs and sheet music were all arranged by artist. He kept his art supplies in a divided bin by his desk and his finished pieces in a portfolio. He knew about every poetry event going on in his hometown and got to each one on time.

The one area in his life that felt out of control was his schoolwork. He lost papers all the time, forgot to write down assignments, and frequently fell behind in his homework. His grades were lower than his potential, and teachers and parents kept telling him he had to get more organized.

The pressure being put on Jack by parents and teachers was not enough to motivate him to get organized. At this point in his life, school was pretty low on Jack's list of priorities. His true joy came from his more creative, independent endeavors—to which he was fully committed. He didn't particularly enjoy school and the last thing he felt like spending his time on was figuring out a better filing system or organizing his study schedule.

When I spoke to Jack, I asked him if doing poorly in school was costing him in any way. He explained that his disorganized approach to schoolwork often got in the way of the things he loves. More than once, he was all set to go to a really important poetry reading when he realized he had a test or paper due the next day and had to stay home to cram. He missed the chance to attend a summer art program at a local museum because he'd failed math and had to go to summer school. And his parents often stopped him from going skateboarding with his buddies until his homework was done.

The good news was that Jack didn't have to convince himself that he loved school; he didn't need to put it higher on his priority list in order to get organized. His motivation to organize his school stuff came from a completely different place—he was driven to have the most time and freedom possible to pursue his creative endeavors.

Once Jack identified the payoff for organizing his school stuff, his organizing systems came together within a couple of weeks. We got him a planner where he kept track of homework assignments and due dates right alongside poetry slams and art classes. His personal mission became to get all his homework done by 6 P.M. on the day it was assigned, freeing his evenings for the fun stuff. He learned how to calculate in advance how long each assignment would take so he could anticipate every opening in his schedule.

Procrastination disappeared, the work got done, and Jack achieved his goal. His grades got better—not the straight A's he might have gotten if school was a higher priority, but a solid B average that satisfied his parents. Most importantly, he now had a predictable study schedule that gave him the freedom he wanted.

Write down the answer for the What's the payoff? question on a notecard or piece of paper. Place the card inside your notebook, wallet, or planner, or post it on the wall where you are working. Anytime in the process you feel like you are about to give up, refer back to this list. A quick glance will remind you why you decided to start organizing in the first place, and it will inspire you to keep going.

Question #4: What's the Problem?

Remember, clutter and time-management problems are not caused by laziness. As discussed in Chapter 1, there are very specific, common reasons we get ourselves into a tangle. The good news is that each one has a solution.

As you tackle each new chapter, refer back to the common-causes list outlined in Chapter 1 to assess your symptoms and determine which combination of factors is causing the problems in the specific area you are about to organize.

By pinpointing the real reasons for the clutter and heading straight to their accompanying solutions, you will save yourself a lot of time and energy. You'll actually solve the problem at its core so that your efforts to get organized are effective and lasting.

STEP 2: STRATEGIZE

OK, you've analyzed your current situation and now understand exactly where you are right now. You are full of new insights and energy, ready to wage a full-scale attack on clutter . . . or are you? Do you know in which direction you are headed?

Moving ahead without a clear vision of your destination is a risky proposition. Imagine trying to get to a party across town with no address, no map, and no sense of how long the trip will take. Getting lost is pretty much guaranteed!

This section will help you navigate the path from chaos to order by showing you how to picture your destination, map out your journey, and realistically estimate how long it will take you to arrive.

In order to successfully strategize any organizing project, we offer you two "secret weapons."

SECRET WEAPON #1: THE KINDERGARTEN MODEL OF ORGANIZATION

Before diving into the piles or messy schedules that are driving you crazy, it helps to visualize what you want your space or schedule to look like once it's finally organized.

Unbeknownst to you, a clear picture of success is stored in your recent memory. Robert Fulghum wrote a best-selling book called *All I Really Need to Know I Learned in Kindergarten*. Well, the same is true of organizing. Walk into any kindergarten classroom in the world and you will behold the perfect model of organization.

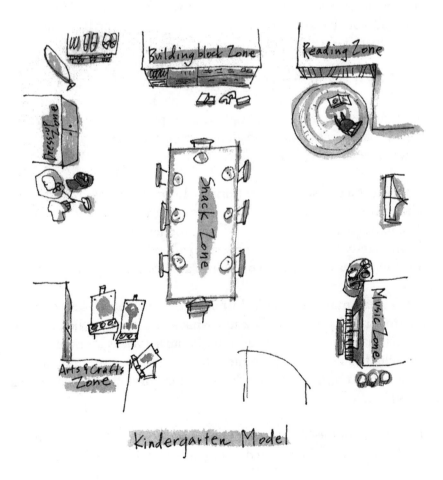

Kindergarten Model

Think about it. No matter how messy that room ever got—and with twenty-five five-year-olds all playing at the same time, it could get pretty messy—when the teacher rang the bell, the room was back in perfect order within one minute.

So, what makes a kindergarten classroom so easy to maintain? There are five key elements:

- **Clearly defined activity zones**. The room is subdivided into clearly marked zones like the Arts and Crafts Zone, the Reading Zone, the Dress-up Zone, the Music Zone, the Snack Zone. As a result, there is only one logical place to find or put away any item.

- **Self-contained spaces**. The zones are so clearly defined and compartmentalized that you can focus 100 percent of your mental energy on one activity at a time. When you are in the reading corner, that's all you are aware of, while kids in the building-block area are lost in that world.

- **Easy-to-access storage**. Everything you need for each activity is stored right where you use it. You don't have to cross the room twenty times to gather supplies to draw a picture. You go straight to the Arts and Crafts Zone and all the crayons, markers, glue, and scissors you ever wanted are at your fingertips.

- **Fun, tactile storage containers**. Every item has a clear, well-labeled home in a container that is the perfect size to hold it. Puzzles slide into slots, scissors are stored in a wooden block with holes, nose down, handles up; smocks hang at eye level on nearby hooks. It's truly almost as much fun to put things away as it is to play with them.

- **Visual map of what's important**. Walk into a kindergarten classroom and you instantly know what's important to the kids who inhabit that space. The layout of the room serves as a visual menu—each child can stand in the center of the room, look around, and see what there is to do without relying on memory about where things are stored.

The beauty of the kindergarten model is that it works for absolutely everything you will ever need to organize. You can use it to organize any physical space in your life—your room, closet, backpack, locker. You can also use it to design your schedule and take control of your time.

There are thousands of executives, artists, businesspeople, and parents all over the world who have based the organization of their homes, offices, filing systems, and schedules on this very simple and effective model.

The simplicity of the kindergarten model frees your mind and time to concentrate on more complicated and interesting things like calculus, your college search, soccer strategies, and your friends. Organizing your spaces into zones gives you only one logical place to put or find anything and sensible times to schedule the various activities in your life. It helps you take control of any situation, giving you more time and space than you ever dreamed you had.

The kindergarten model is an integral part of turning organizing into a form of self-expression. Spaces designed on this model reveal a lot about the person who inhabits the space. Your space and your time become a visual reflection of what's important to you and keep you grounded in a constantly changing world.

Throughout the rest of this book, you'll see examples for tailoring each area of your life along the lines of the kindergarten model of organization. Part 2 will show you how to apply the kindergarten model to your physical space. Part 3 will demonstrate how to apply it to time.

SECRET WEAPON #2: ESTIMATE THE TIME

One of the biggest mistakes many people make when it comes to organizing is being completely unrealistic about how long the job will take. Most people either dramatically overestimate or drastically underestimate the time required.

If you overestimate the job, chances are you'll never get started. For example, if you think it'll take a month to organize your room, you'll end up putting it off forever. If you think it will take an hour to take out the garbage, you may procrastinate another four hours before you begin. On the other hand, underestimating the time will kill your chances of successful completion as well. You think, "I'll tackle this in an hour Sunday morning before I go to the mall," but when shopping time arrives and you find that you're nowhere near finishing, you drop the job like a hot potato.

One of the most valuable organizing skills to acquire is the ability to realistically calculate how long things will take. Each specific project requires a different amount of time, obviously, and each person works at a different pace. However, by learning to ask the question of how long projects take, you can better plan your time and have the success you want.

For example, here is a list of the main organizing projects in this book. Try to estimate how long each one would take you to do.

⏱ How Long Will It Take?

Take a guess at how long each of the following organizing projects will take you. Then check against the answer key below.

A. Bedroom _____
B. Closet _____
C. School Papers _____
D. Locker _____
E. Backpack _____
F. Memorabilia _____
G. Collections _____
H. Schedule _____

(Answers: A: 5–8 hrs; B: 2–4 hrs; C: 2–3 hrs; D: ½–1 hr; E: ½–1 hr; F: 3–5 hrs; G: 1–3 hrs; H: 1–2 hrs)

Is It Worth the Time?

At this point, you may be having second thoughts about this whole organizing thing; you may be wondering whether the time required is worth the investment.

FACT: Studies show that most people lose an average of one to two hours per day due to disorganization: time wasted when searching for misplaced items, procrastinating on overwhelming tasks, or wondering what to do next. Based on that math, getting organized could free an additional seven to fourteen hours per week. Wouldn't that take some of the stress off? What would you do with that extra time? If you had seven to fourteen hours per week, how would you spend it?

Fill in: _____

STEP 3: ATTACK

Congratulations! You've analyzed and strategized . . . and now you are finally ready to dive in and conquer the clutter. It's time to sort through the mountains of stuff in your space and weed through the problems in your schedule to create the organized life you desire.

So, how do you do it? Tackling those mounds is overwhelming only when you don't know where to start. If you don't know how to get organized, of course it feels overwhelming—that's the nature of being a beginner. Just remember your first day at your new school: You

%   Let's look at what the disorder is costing you.

- One out of every three U.S. teens reports feeling stress on a daily basis.
- In a *Teen* magazine survey, 74 percent of girls said that their teen years are more stressful than those of their parents.
- Sixty-eight percent describe their fellow teens as generally "really" or "kind of" stressed. Fifty-eight percent say this stress is due to being over-scheduled.
- Sixty-two percent of high school students feel they are always or frequently rushed to keep up with high school, jobs, family, and social lives.
- Forty-three percent said they would like to increase the amount of time spent with family.
- Sixty-eight percent would like to improve their grades.
- Sixty-eight percent would like to get more exercise.

probably thought you'd never figure out how to get from your locker to your classes without missing the bell.

Part 2 is devoted to organizing spaces. Part 3 is all about time management. The "Attack" phase includes special steps and tools that vary depending on what you are organizing. Knowing what those tools are will make the "Attack" stage less overwhelming and keep you from falling into traps that prevent you from succeeding.

ATTACKING SPACE

In Chapter 3, you'll discover the special tools, supplies, and techniques for organizing spaces, including the SPACE formula for digging through your piles of stuff:

Sort
Purge
Assign a home
Containerize
Equalize

ATTACKING TIME

Chapter 7 will provide you with the special tools, supplies, and techniques for time management, including the WADE formula for sorting through the zillions of choices you have to make on any given day.

Write it down
Add it up
Decide when
Execute your plan

Where should you start? Some people prefer to organize space first, because it's visual, dramatic, and energizing. On the other hand, spending an hour or two rearranging your schedule first will free up time to spend on a bigger organizing project.

Start with the area that is bothering you the most. It will give you the quickest sense of accomplishment.

Armed with the three-step process of Analyze, Strategize, Attack, you are about to discover how easy it is to get organized. Once you master the steps, you'll see that they really do boil down to a simple and predictable process. When broken down, it isn't overwhelming anymore and can, in fact, actually be enjoyable. Using the strategies laid out in this book, you can speed up and simplify the organizing process. You are about to make your organizing dreams come true.

Are you ready? Let's go.

PART 2

Organizing
Your Space

3

Tools for Organizing Your Space and Stuff

- 💬 "I can never find things when I need them."–Heidi S., 16, Michigan

- 💬 "I can't keep my room clean. It's so messy and overwhelming."–Caitlin L., 13, Iowa

- 💬 "I'm always losing my glasses, keys, and wallet–it's caused me serious problems sometimes."–Jonathan D., 15, New York

There are very few rules in this book, but the most important one is this: *Make sure you've read Chapters 1 and 2 before going any further!* The first part of this book provides the foundation for every organizing project you'll ever take on. Whether you're trying to organize your room, your memorabilia, your locker, or your school stuff, it's easy to get sidetracked and overwhelmed. Skipping the basics will only make things worse. So if you've thought you'd just jump ahead to the "good stuff," think again–and go back to page 3.

If there's one thing all teens have in common, it's the immense amount of stuff they have in their bedrooms, lockers, and backpacks. Keeping all of your things in order isn't easy. But we're here to tell you that organizing your stuff and space doesn't have to be an overwhelming chore.

This chapter will show you how to master your space and stuff by equipping you with the three basic tools for organizing success.

The Three Basic Tools for Organizing Your Space and Stuff

In the battle for control of your space and stuff, you'll need to be armed with the three basic tools:

1. Supplies checklist
2. SPACE formula
3. Rules for visible, dramatic, results

TOOL #1: SUPPLIES CHECKLIST

Nothing is more annoying than having to stop in the middle of the job in search of garbage bags or cleaning materials while you're still up to your elbows in the class notes you took two years ago. **Assemble your supplies first**. Here's a checklist of the supplies you're likely to need:

_____ **Large, strong trash bags** to hold the weight of stuff you're tossing

_____ **3 large boxes or containers**, labeled as follows:

Give away—Use a separate box for each destination if you will be giving things to more than one place.

Belongs elsewhere—Place items that belong in another location in this box to distribute at the conclusion of your organizing session.

Needs repair—Use this box for any items you want to keep that need fixing, such as broken in-line skates. Label the box with a deadline—such as two weeks or a month from the present date—for repairs. If you haven't gotten the items back into working order by then, it's time to let them go.

_____ **Dust buster, dust cloth, spray cleaner, broom, and dustpan**—Emptied shelves and drawers provide a prime opportunity for deep cleaning not to be missed.

_____ **Markers and Post-its or labels** for labeling boxes and groups of items as you sort

_____ **Notepad and pen** for writing down future or follow-up projects

OPTIONAL:

_____ **Label maker**

_____ **Box of plain or colored manila folders** (if you are sorting papers)

TOOL #2: SPACE FORMULA—PUTTING IT ALL TOGETHER

After you have analyzed and strategized, you'll be ready to roll up your sleeves, dig into those piles, and start creating some order. At the end of Part 1, we introduced the SPACE formula. Now you'll learn how it works. Are you ready? Let's break down the formula!

S.P.A.C.E.

Sort—Go through each possession and group of similar items.

Purge—Get rid of the duplicates, excess, undesirable, and irrelevant.

Assign a home—Decide where each item you are keeping will live.

Containerize—Use bins, baskets, and cubbies to keep categories separate and make cleanup a breeze.

Equalize—Maintain and update your system to keep up with your changing interests, needs, and priorities.

The key to succeeding with the SPACE formula is to complete *every one* of the steps and, most important, to complete them *in order*. Some of these steps may sound familiar to you. But chances are that in the past you followed only a few of them, and not necessarily in their proper order. Out of sequence, these actions aren't effective—you'll see why in a minute.

Let's look at each critical step and figure out how it all works.

Sort

When you are disorganized, your belongings are usually all mixed up, often scattered in multiple locations. For example, you may have shoes under your bed, in your closet, in the hall, and under the kitchen table. The first step in creating a sense of order is to go through your possessions and divide them into groups of similar items.

You'll need to clear an area for the actual sorting—the floor, the bed, or a tabletop will do. Next, examine every item you pick up and evaluate it individually, asking yourself: What is this item? What category does it belong in?

Although you shouldn't focus on getting rid of things right now, if you do come across something that's just begging to be tossed, feel free to indulge the impulse. Otherwise, concentrate exclusively on sorting and use the following guidelines to help the process along:

• *Group the way you think:* As you identify items, place them in related categories that reflect *your* associations. The categories only have to make sense to you. Some people may choose to categorize their closets by season. Others may prefer to organize by function: everyday clothes in one section, sports clothes in another, and fancy dress clothes in a third.

• *Keep your categories manageable:* If you end up creating fifty piles with only one or two items in each, you are overcategorizing, a situation that will make your system too hard to remember, let alone maintain. Look the piles over and see which ones could be combined because of their relationship to each other (for example, if you have three regular T-shirts and five long-sleeve T-shirts, group them all into one category called T-shirts). On the other hand, if everything you pick up gets grouped into just a couple of towering piles (clothes in one huge stack, schoolbooks and papers in another, music in a third), try to subdivide the big stacks to make them less cumbersome. For example, subdivide clothes by type; break down school stuff into books, supplies, and papers; and separate music by genre.

• *It's absolutely crucial that you evaluate everything:* Don't put off or ignore those large piles of stuff in the corner or scattered pockets of clutter that seem too intimidating. Skipping them or putting them off for some other time will prevent you from seeing the big picture *before* you set up your system. And unsorted piles will eventually degenerate your system.

Purge

Now that all your worldly possessions are gathered and grouped
into categories, you can see
exactly how much and what
you have. This should make
the next step a little easier:
deciding what to get rid
of and how. That's
because once you've
completed the sort-
ing process, you
may find that you
have more stuff
in a single category
than you'll ever use
(e.g., twenty bottles of sham-
poo or thirty-two identical pairs of jeans).

There are always some candidates for automatic tossing, otherwise known as no-brainers. These are items that are in such bad shape, and so irrelevant in your life right now, that you couldn't or wouldn't use them if you wanted to (dried-out markers, inkless pens, crumpled wrapping paper from a gift you got three years ago). Each chapter from here on out will include a "No-Brainer Toss List" to get you started.

Other items may pose tougher choices. For instance, maybe all fifty-six white T-shirts are in decent shape. In that case, grab what you need, pick your favorites, and toss the rest.

It may still be hard to part with things. Guilt—"But that was so expensive"—and sentimentality—"But that was a gift from a friend, even though I don't like it"—can make it really hard to say good-bye.

How do you motivate yourself to get rid of the excess, the unnec-
essary, the irrelevant, the duplicates, the triplicates, the broken, the stained, and the torn? Here are some tips to make the parting easier.

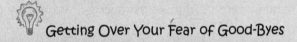

Getting Over Your Fear of Good-Byes

- *Keep only what you use and love.* Everything else becomes a barrier between you and what you need to get to every day. Let go of items that *used* to be important to you or you thought *might be* important to you someday.
- *Focus on the positive.* Instead of thinking about what you are getting rid of, remember what you are gaining: space—for the things you really use and love; time—to do things other than search through clutter; freedom—because being organized enables you to be more responsible; and growth—purging gives new aspects of your personality room to develop.
- *Adopt a charity (or a friend).* Share the items you no longer need or bought but never used. It's a lot easier to part with things that are still in good shape when you know they will be put to good use by someone else. Find a church, synagogue, children's hospital, homeless shelter, or other organization that would love your giveaways. If you have friends who wear your size, maybe they'd be happy to adopt the things you bought that aren't really quite you.
- *Host a swap party.* One person's trash is another's treasure. Invite your friends to bring all their castaways to a party at your house, dump it all on the floor in the living room, and let the trading begin. Leftovers can go to a mutually agreed-upon charity.
- *Have a tag sale or visit a consignment shop.* If money motivates you, think about having a garage sale or bringing your stuff to a resale shop. This way, as you clean out your stuff, you won't think of it as losing a jacket you never wear, but as making fifteen dollars you can put toward a new set of skis.
- *Put it in storage.* If you have things you aren't using right now but can't bear to part with permanently just yet, consider boxing them up and storing them elsewhere—in the attic, the basement, the guest-room closet, or wherever your parents will let you. Label your boxes carefully and keep an inventory of everything you store so you'll remember what you put away and know where to find it.

Assign a Home

Since each item needs a home, it's time to take all the stuff that you've decided to keep and figure out precisely where you're going to put it—which shelf, drawer, or section of your locker. Where will it live so that you always know where to put it and where to find it?

One of the keys to assigning homes is to store items where they're used instead of simply where they fit. For example, if you read books before you go to sleep, place a bookcase close to your bed.

Most important when tackling this step is to steer clear of inconsistency. "Well, I'll sometimes put my calculator here, and sometimes keep it in my backpack." Apply the "Select One" rule—that is, give each item one single, consistent home, always keeping in mind the relationship of one category to another. For example, in your CD rack you may put rock next to club music, because both are good for dancing.

While you're going about assigning homes, you may find that you don't have enough space to accommodate all the different objects. In this case, you have two options: try to purge more stuff (perhaps by relocating or getting rid of a few extra duplicates) or maximize your storage space. Chapters 4, 5, and 6 will provide you with ideas for expanding your current storage space and tips for finding storage possibilities where none seems to exist.

Containerize

At long last, you've reached the fun part! You've been waiting patiently and resisting the temptation to shop for containers for what sometimes felt like centuries. Well, you've been patient long enough. Now the time has come where we get to personalize your space with cool-looking gadgets, gizmos, baskets, and bins.

Containers keep your categories of items grouped and separated, making retrieval, cleanup, and maintenance a breeze. Containers also help set limits on how much you accumulate in any given category because you can keep only as much as the container will hold. And, best of all, they allow you to get creative and infuse your system with your personal style.

We'll make general recommendations for the types and sizes of containers needed for each individual organizing job. You may already have all the containers you need around the house. If not, places to find inexpensive containers include hardware stores (check the kitchen and closet departments!), art-supply stores, flea markets, even flower suppliers. Consider decorating your storage containers with contact paper, paint, and markers.

And voilà—you're done! Well, almost . . .

Equalize

Nothing is forever, as they say. Just because you're wearing a size 6 sneaker now doesn't mean that you'll be wearing size 6 sneakers forever. You're going to grow and your feet will change, and if you don't periodically go back to the store to see what new size you need, your toes will be poking through those size 6's and they're going to be mighty uncomfortable.

It's the same with organizing. You can't expect any given system to work forever. It will have to be monitored and updated regularly to keep up with your changing interests, needs, and priorities. Once you've laid out your system, you'll need to maintain it. That's what "equalizing" is all about.

Initial Checkup

About two weeks after you've designed your system, you'll want to evaluate how it has been performing. Is everything as easy as you would like it to be? Do the zones and categories you set up still make sense? Are there any rough spots that need to be smoothed out? Chances are, you'll need to make more than a few minor adjustments before your system is a comfy fit.

Once everything is running smoothly, you need to set in place daily and periodic maintenance routines to ensure the balance. Keep it simple. If a maintenance program is too time-consuming and complex, you won't follow it.

Daily Cleanup

Select a set time every day for cleanup. Remember how magical and fast it was in kindergarten? Now, no matter how messy your space gets over the course of the day, it should not take more than three to five minutes to tidy up because everything has a logical, accessible, and identifiable home. The time you choose for this activity is up to you—it could be right before dinner, right before bed, or as soon as you wake up in the morning. The key is to pick a time that feels right and make it a routine. Then just do it until it becomes a habit.

Seasonal Tune-Ups

Periodic tune-ups are necessary to keep your system in sync with the changes—big and small—in your life. You should schedule appointments with yourself once a year to evaluate whether your system is still working. It's an important opportunity to make adjustments for any new items you've acquired, purge old things that you no longer need or want, and even integrate a new organizing technique or gadget into your system to keep it fresh and fun.

TOOL #3: RULES FOR VISIBLE, DRAMATIC RESULTS

The more stuff you have, the easier it will be to get overwhelmed by the job at hand. Applying the following rules will help you get instant results and feel an encouraging sense of progress as you work.

Rule #1: Attack What's Visible First

Although it seems logical to begin by cleaning out the clutter in your drawers, cabinets, and closets to make room for the stuff on the surfaces, this is a major mistake. Instead of decreasing the piles, you'll be adding to them—a very discouraging sight. The stuff hidden away is usually old and irrelevant anyway.

By attacking the visible surface clutter first, you'll take instant control of the things you use every day—and within an hour or so, you'll be feeling energized by your progress.

Rule #2: Use the Quick-Sort Plan

This technique keeps you moving through your stuff swiftly. Focus solely on identifying and categorizing your objects into groups (sports equipment, memorabilia, etc.) without belaboring decisions about what to keep and what to toss. However, if a decision to toss something *does* come easily, great—one less item to worry about. If not, sort the item and move on.

Rule #3: Don't Play Catch-Up

As you organize, you will undoubtedly unearth lots of unfinished to-dos (incomplete letters, overdue library books, unread articles, etc.). This is not the time to catch up. Instead, create a "Future Projects" list and schedule a separate time to deal with them later.

Rule #4: Avoid Zigzag Organizing

Avoid the mistake of scattering your organizing efforts, working back and forth between several spaces at once. If you have started in your closet, complete that area before moving on to the bookshelves, desk area, or bedside.

Working one section at a time will enable you to visualize your progress, give you natural places to take breaks, and reward you with many small victories along the way.

Rule #5: Play Beat-the-Clock

Try setting reasonable time limits for how long you want to spend on each individual job and speed up your efforts if you see that you're lagging behind. One fun way to play beat-the-clock is by working to the sounds of your favorite CDs and challenging yourself to sort each section (bookcase, closet, nightstand, etc.) by the time the CD is finished.

Like anything else worth doing, organization takes time to master. You're bound to make mistakes and stumble along the way. When you do, simply relax, take a deep breath, and hop back on track.

Once you've mastered the three basic tools, they'll last forever. That's their greatest value: You can apply what you learn over and over again, to virtually any task. And they will give you a lasting sense of security, personal identity, pride, and peace of mind.

Planning Your Organizing Priorities

Don't try to organize everything all at once. Based on the self-assessment you did in the last chapter, decide what areas need organizing and in which order you'd like to fix them. Keep in mind the demands of your schedule, and be realistic. Tackling more than one project a month is probably not a good idea.

The main thing is to get it right, continue to live your life, and enjoy your progress. Where should you begin? Starting with the area that is bothering you the most is often the best approach, as it affords the greatest sense of accomplishment. List your priorities below.

Priority #	Space	See Chapter
____	Bedroom	4
____	Closet	4
____	School papers	5
____	Backpack	5
____	Locker	5
____	Memorabilia	6
____	Photos	6
____	Collections	6

4

The Bedroom

Project Checklist	
MATERIALS	Large, strong trash bags
	3 large boxes labeled "give away," "belongs elsewhere," and "needs repair"
	Dust cloth and spray
	Broom and dustpan
	Notepad for tracking future projects
	Storage containers (to be selected later in process)
	Label maker or marker and labels
ESTIMATED TIME	Bedroom 5–8 hours
	Closet 2–4 hours

The bedroom is so much more than just a place to sleep. It's your main headquarters, your sanctuary, the room where you can talk on the phone for hours, do your homework in peace and quiet, and escape the noise, distractions, and pressures of the world around you. Your bedroom is an extension of who you are and the space where you can express yourself freely.

Still, most teens cite their bedrooms as one of the most disorganized areas in their lives. Keeping that space organized can seem like an impossible challenge. Right now, your room is probably cluttered with an overwhelming combination of things that *used to be* important, things that you thought *might be important,* and things that are actually *important to you right now.* The majority of your room should be occupied by what is essential *to you right now*.

As you organize your room, you will come across many categories of items. School stuff, photos, collections, and memorabilia can be so involved when it comes to organizing that we've set aside separate whole chapters to deal with them. Feel free to set those items apart, to be tackled on another day.

Depending on the size of your wardrobe, some people also find it easier to tackle clothing on one day and the rest of the room on another. For example, if you have clothes scattered all over the floor, gather them up, toss them into your closet, and deal with them when you are ready to take on the closet area. Or start with your closet and do the rest of the room at another time.

The keys to making your room work for you are all laid out in this section. If you follow these simple steps and suggestions, you will enjoy all the rewards, relaxation, and sense of empowerment that come with a well-organized bedroom that reflects who you are and what you need.

PHASE 1: ANALYZE

Get out a pen and a notebook and prepare to do some serious thinking. Answer the following four questions thoughtfully and thoroughly. Your answers will be instrumental in coming up with a blueprint for the perfect reorganization of your room.

Question #1: What's Working and What's Not?

 💬 "I have a lamp on my nightstand so I never have to get out of bed to turn off the light when I'm reading and about to fall asleep."   —Orrin P., 15, Maryland

💬 "I have everyone on speed dial. I never have to search for a number."   —Martha H., 16, New York

💬 "My room is covered in clothes. I can't make one move without stepping on a sweater or a T-shirt."

—Adam R., 16, Iowa

💬 "I bought a bunch of containers to keep all my stuff in. Now they're so crammed with stuff that I never even want to look inside them."   —Joshy B., 17, Minnesota

Put a plus (+) next to what's working and a minus (−) next to what's not.

(+) (−)		(+) (−)	
_____	Clothes	_____	Memorabilia*
_____	Shoes	_____	Furniture arrangement
_____	Accessories	_____	Photos*
_____	Videos and DVDs	_____	Books
_____	Closet	_____	School stuff (desk, papers,
_____	Bedside area		etc.)**
_____	Lighting	_____	Decorations
		_____	CDs

More what's working:

_____

_____

_____

More what's *not* working:

_____

_____

_____

* See chapter 6.
** See chapter 5.

Question #2: What's Your Essential 7?

Before diving into the clutter, take a step back and ask yourself what are the true essentials—the things that you use and enjoy the most, the items that help define your room. Your Essential 7 help make your room unique and they reveal a lot about who you are. By figuring out your Essential 7, you'll be one step closer to identifying what's really important to you.

For example, if you chose your books as one of the Essential 7, reading is probably very important to you. If you chose awards and trophies, you put a high premium on academic achievement or sports.

The Bedroom Essential 7 for Four Different Teens

Marieke S., 14, New York	Sam O., 15, Missouri	Amanda L., 14, Massachusetts	Jessica S., 18, Ohio
1. butterfly plate my grandma gave me 2. card with twenty four-leaf clovers 3. perfume bottle from Milan trip with Mom 4. self-portrait watercolor I made when two 5. baby quilt 6. art portfolio 7. four-leaf clover medallion	1. computer 2. math awards 3. dresser 4. mirror 5. dictionary 6. alarm clock 7. stereo	1. Bible 2. phone 3. phone book 4. photos of friends and family 5. bed 6. snow globes 7. teddy bear	1. angels 2. quilt my grandma made me 3. clothes 4. jewelry 5. nail polish/makeup supplies 7. books

Question #3: What's the Payoff?

Organizing your room takes time, determination, and—let's face it—a good dose of courage. There are a lot of decisions to make and it won't happen overnight. It may be the space that takes the longest to organize, especially if it's been a wreck for a long time. Now is the time to identify what you hope to gain by organizing your room. The more specific you can be with your payoff, the more motivated you will be to start and finish the job.

> ● "My goal in organizing my room is to feel in control and on top of things."   —Scott G., 15, Iowa

> ● "I'd like to organize my closet so that I can find my clothes more easily and look better when I go to school."
> —Mary S., 16, Virginia

💬 "I want to get organized to keep better track of stuff and stop my sisters from borrowing my things without my permission."   —Jennifer Q., 15, Texas

💬 "I make handcrafted jewelry and would be able to do more if I had a space for all of my supplies."
                                        —Abby A., 17, New Mexico

Jessi Says

What's My Payoff?

My bedroom is my home base and keeping it organized is a must. If my room isn't in solid condition, it's difficult to keep the rest of my life on track. Here are some other reasons that motivate me to keep my room organized.

My room is the only space on the entire planet that is solely mine. Over the past sixteen years, I have collected a tremendous amount of stuff that I love and want to hold on to. Keeping my room in order minimizes the space that my things take up and allows me to bring more of what I want into my life.

My organized room allows me to maximize my space and time. If I have to make a display for a school project, and my room is in order, I can go in and get right to work.

My room boosts my confidence. In such a competitive world, it's comforting to know that I have myself together from the ground up (my room). It gives me confidence to know that I am on top of my game.

My room gives others (especially my mom!) confidence in me. An organized room tells the world that you have it all together. My mom is more comfortable in giving me my space and freedom because she knows that I can take care of myself.

Organizing my room allows me to do what I want, when I want. If I want to meditate with music, candles, and incense, it takes only a minute to get the aura going. My full collection of scents and my CDs are right where I need them.

Question #4: What's the Problem?

Each person has a unique combination of causes for the clutter in his or her room. Check the boxes next to those problems that may be affecting you.

❑ Homeless items	❑ More stuff than space	❑ Sentimental attachments
❑ Inconvenient storage	❑ Unappealing space	❑ Lack of confidence
❑ Complex, confusing system	❑ Disorganized family	❑ Fear of losing individuality
❑ "Out of sight, out of mind" mentality	❑ "Organizing is boring" mind-set	❑ Unclear goals and priorities

✎ Julie's Work Journal:

Lena's Story

When Lena's family moved, her new room was much smaller than her old one. Actually, it was half its size. Lena, a seventeen-year-old cross-country runner, was very unhappy about this situation and never took the time to pull this new room together. Finally, her parents sent her to me for a consultation.

During my work with Lena, we diagnosed the combination of clutter culprits in her room. These were: (1) more stuff than storage, (2) homeless items, (3) unappealing space, and (4) sentimental attachments.

When she couldn't take it anymore, Lena got organized by (1) focusing on the essentials and paring down her stuff to include only what she used regularly and loved and (2) increasing storage by adding underbed bins on wheels, a rack on the back of her bedroom door, and a three-tiered stacking drawer unit to replace her simple nightstand. She also stenciled a border around the room to make it prettier and added a small fish tank.

Finally, to display her memorabilia without taking up too much space, she asked her dad to build a shelf that ran close to the ceiling around the whole room to showcase her Winnie the Pooh collection and running trophies.

PHASE 2: STRATEGIZE

 Map Out a Plan!

So, how do you transform your current state of bedroom chaos into the kindergarten model of organization? The answer is as easy as one, two, three. Take out a pencil, a couple of sheets of paper, and start designing!

Task #1: Define Your Activities

Ask yourself: How do I fill my time? What are the main activities that I perform in my room? Write these down, as they will become the foundation of your zone design.

Be cautious in planning your zones. Limit your list to a maximum of three to five main activities to keep your room from becoming overcrowded, overwhelming, and hard to manage.

In addition to activity zones, you might also consider display zones that house your

- collections (candles, bootleg concert tapes, model cars, dolls, etc.)
- memorabilia (photos of friends, theater tickets, autographs, etc.)
- artwork (posters, paintings, decorations, homemade videos, etc.)
- trophies and awards

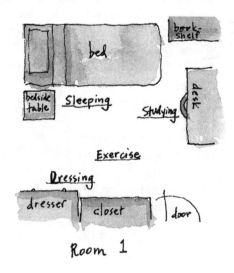

Room 1

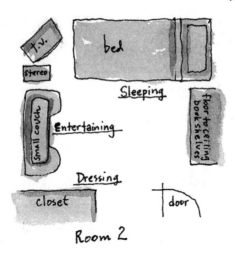

Room 2

Task #2: Mix 'n' Match Zone Planner

Now it's time to figure out which elements belong in each zone. Divide a sheet of paper into three columns labeled "zones," "supplies," and "storage units."

First, list all the zones that you'll need in your room. Assign a letter to each zone (A, B, C, etc.). In the column labeled "supplies," list all of the supplies you use for each activity. In the third column, marked "storage units," list all of the possible containers you already own that can be used to store your supplies.

Use the following partially completed example as a starting place.

Zones	Supplies	Storage Units
A-Reading	**A**-Books	**A**-Nightstand
B-TV/music	**A**-Magazines	**A**-Desk
Dressing	**A**-School stuff	**A**-Bookcase
Studying	Hanging clothes	Dresser
Sleeping	Folded pants, sweaters	Closet
	B-CDs	Closet shelves
	Brush and hair products	Bed
	B-Stereo and headphones	Underbed storage
	Shoes	**B**-TV/stereo stand
	Camp stuff	**B**-CD cases
	B-TV guide	Crates
	B-Remote Control	*Add your own here:*
	Add your own here:	

Some storage units may do double duty, storing supplies for more than one activity, due to their location. If a storage unit, let's say a nightstand, has more than three zones' letters by it, you may need to reconsider your arrangement—chances are good that you're cramming too much stuff into it or trying to make it serve too many different, and possibly competing, uses.

Teen Inventory

Ever wonder what other teens are storing in their rooms? We've inventoried the rooms of four different teens. The results are in.

Heli S., 14	Tiffany T., 15	Gilli C., 14	Casey K., 16
100 books	24 books	78 books	50 T-shirts
50 CDs	18 stuffed animals	25 CDs	13 jeans/pants
50 stuffed animals	17 CDs	15 video games	14 stuffed animals
10 T-shirts	12 T-shirts	14 stuffed	65 CDs
7 jeans/pants	5 school	animals	3 pairs of
5 video games	notebooks	14 T-shirts	sneakers
5 photo albums	5 jeans/pants	6 school	too many books
3 pairs of	5 pairs of	notebooks	6 photo albums
sneakers	sneakers	5 photo albums	3 *Harry Potter*
2 posters	3 photo albums	5 jeans/pants	books
2 school		5 pairs of	
notebooks		sneakers	

Personal Inventory

How many of each item do you currently own? (example, CDs: *25*, Pairs of sneakers: *12*, etc.)

CDs _____	Photo albums _____	Videos/DVDs _____
Pairs of sneakers _____	Stuffed animals _____	Bags _____
T-shirts _____	Posters _____	Candles _____
Pairs of socks _____	Sports equipment _____	Pairs of shoes _____
Books _____	Video games _____	Pants _____
Old notebooks _____	Miscellaneous collections _____	Tops _____

Task #3: Plan Your Layout

On a second piece of paper, using a pencil, draw a map of your room. Indicate doors and windows and any other key architectural features. Your drawing does not have to be a masterpiece.

Now, it's time to sketch out some ideas for rearranging the space to create activity zones.

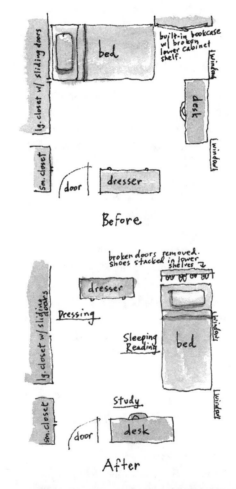

Before

After

Before	After
• messy room • clothes everywhere • no place to study • no zones	• zones planned out • reading supplies next to bed • clothes organized in closet

Special Circumstances:
SHARING A BEDROOM

If you share a room with a sibling, you know how limited or nonexistent your space can seem. But there's no reason why sharing a room should hamper your sense of individuality or take away your privacy. Here are some ideas for making the most of your shared room:

Space
- If you have two single beds, use folding screens to attractively separate areas.
- Place tall bookcases back-to-back in the middle of the room to separate the room and provide privacy.
- If you have bunk beds (or even if you don't), divide the rest of the room into three distinct zones—sibling 1, sibling 2, and shared zones.

Clothes
- If there are two closets, assign one to each sibling, or designate one closet for dress clothes, the other for school clothes, and divide each closet in half.
- If there's only one closet and it's too small to share, consider giving one sibling the closet and the dressers to the other.
- Use colored plastic hangers to distinguish your clothes from your sibling's. Also, initial the inside tag of garments with laundry pens.
- Place dressers next to your closets in your bedroom to create a convenient pair of Dressing Zones.

Moving Furniture

STOP Once you've planned your layout, it's time to roll up your sleeves and make the magic happen. Start rearranging furniture to make your zones come alive. But not so fast! Before you move anything, remember to ask your parents first. Furniture can be very heavy, and you can hurt yourself, the walls, the floor, or the furniture if you go it alone. Get permission and get help.

Once you've received the go-ahead, you can start moving furniture and storage units around to fit your vision and watch as your zones come to life.

You'll actually see what fits where and how you like it there. This will allow you to make the necessary adjustments. The instant transformation is extremely motivating and will boost your enthusiasm for following your organizing project through to the end.

Special Circumstances:
SMALL BEDROOM

Ideas for Stretching Space

Is your room too small to fit your zone needs? Try these quick and easy space-savers.

- Store off-season clothing, extra shoes, or memorabilia in containers that roll under the bed.
- Use bedside furniture that also provides storage. For example, a small three-drawer dresser can serve as a bedside table as well as storage for your journal, projects-in-progress, reading material, and Walkman.
- Drape a piece of fabric over a folding table to add a new surface for a stereo or computer with concealed storage space below.
- Store exercise clothes and dance or sports gear at the foot of your bed in a space-saving chest or trunk.
- No room for a bedside table? Mount shelves above or beside your bed for books, reading material, and your alarm clock.
- Decorate vertically! Instead of cluttering the surface of your desk or dresser top with figurines and photos, get a wall display or hang shelves near the ceiling.
- Appeal to your parents for a loft or bunk bed. There are loft futons that give you a sofa below and sleeping loft above.
- Put two small bookcases back-to-back to create a sleeping area on one side, a desk/homework area on the other.
- Place the bed or desk perpendicular to the wall or in the center of the room to create a natural room divider. Note: Centering or angling your bed also makes it easier to make your bed.
- Move your dresser next to the closet to make a convenient Dressing Zone.
- Don't feel constrained by outlets and phone jacks—that's what extension cords are for. But check with your parents first and use surge protectors for safety.

Special Circumstances:
SMALL CLOSET SPACE

Stretching Closet Space

Ever since people first had closet space, they've complained not having enough closet space. With all due respect to the architects and contractors of the world, a single high shelf with one hanging rod is not very practical, and many closets are so tiny or oddly shaped, it's a challenge to fit *anything* inside.

Most people don't know how to make the most of their closet space. Things get thrown around in a haphazard way, creating a big black hole—things go in, but they don't come out. It takes a lot of skill to maximize every inch of closet space. Here are some handy ideas, no matter what type of closet challenge you are facing:

Group long hanging garments on one end of the rod and short hanging garments on the other to open up space for a small dresser or large shoe rack.

If you don't have many clothes to hang, fill the space beneath the pole with a dresser.

Remove sliding doors for better access to all of your clothes at once.

Solve the nightmare of a double-deep closet by using the back rod for off-season clothing.

Or remove the front rod entirely; install side shelves for sweaters, shoes, folded wear, bags, and accessories in its place; reserve the remaining back rod for all your hanging garments.

STOP Closet too shallow to hang anything? Remove the rod altogether and install shelves for storing folded garments.

Double your storage space by double-hanging your clothing rods. Tension rods and special hanging double-rods make installation easy.

STOP *Rod and shelves too high? Measure your longest hanging garment and lower the rod so that the garment falls one inch above the floor. (Note: It's a good idea to install a low-pile rug or carpet to keep clothes dust free.) Add shelves above the rod for eye-level access. This is easier said than done, so ask your parents if you need help.*

Big closet, tiny door? Change the direction of the rods to convert a bad situation into a mini walk-in closet.

Too much space between shelves? Add extra shelves or look for containers that can double the available space.

PHASE 3: ATTACK

Step 1: Sort

Clear some space on the floor and/or the bed for sorting onto. You may need to box up piles of unsorted items to make room. Then, focusing on one area or box at a time, remember to apply the technique of quick-sort, quickly defining what each object is and sorting it into a group rather than belaboring the decision of what to keep or toss. Also, don't forget to stick to the task at hand. When you come upon unfinished to-dos, add them to your running list of future projects and stay focused on the sorting process until you complete your inventory.

Of course, in the beginning it makes sense to sort by broad categories (e.g., CDs, school papers, books), but as the piles get larger, you may need to subdivide to keep things manageable.

POSSIBLE CATEGORIES

Here are some subcategories to consider adopting when the categories themselves grow too large. Choose from the list provided or feel free to create your own.

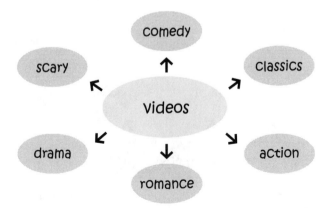

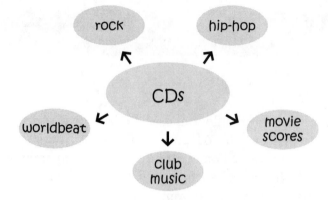

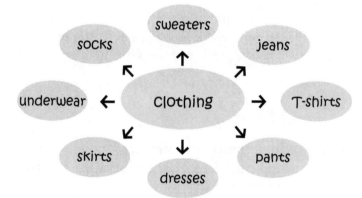

Step 2: Purge

Now that you see how much you have in each category, it's time to get rid of the extras, the duplicates, triplicates, broken, stained, and useless.

Even those of you who find it nearly impossible to say good-bye to your favorite Backstreet Boys or Britney T-shirt can accomplish this step by accentuating the positive. Don't worry so much about what to throw away. You can hold on to anything you want, just as long as it's something you use regularly or adore.

Remember that anything you keep that doesn't fit one of these two criteria forms a barrier that you have to climb over, dig under, or shove aside to get to what you use and love every day. With certain items, you may find that you no longer use them, but you still love them—typically these fall under the heading of memorabilia or decorations. This category is so important we've written a whole chapter about it (see Chapter 6). For now, though, box up those nostalgic indulgences and set them aside until we get to that chapter.

🗑 The No-Brainer Toss List

No need to think twice about this list. To make room for your more important possessions, let these go:

- Old books and teen magazines you've read and will never read again
- The reindeer sweater your next-door neighbor got you that you never wore
- The broken bell from your old bicycle
- Old wire hangers that are bent out of shape
- The wood-shop project you never finished, never liked, and couldn't care less about

Step 3: Assign a Home

A successful purge should leave you with a lot fewer items than when you started. Now, it's time to assign a single, consistent home for each category of items you've decided to keep. Be sure to keep your zones in mind. Using the following guidelines, match up each pile of keepers with a fitting location in your room.

Jessi Says

Cleaning Out My Closet

Every six months or so, after finishing a huge laundry load, I go to put my clothes back in the closet and find that my closet drawers are already full. How can this be? I ask myself. If I just finished cleaning all of the clothes I ever wear, what is all this stuff doing in my closet? Then it dawns on me that the clothes that are still in my closet are all old, uncared-for clothes that I don't want anymore. Time to clean out my closet!

The massive backup of ignored clothing creeps up on me because I get sentimental about clothes that were given to me or that I wore on a special occasion. It can be hard to part with the memories. I also worry that I might need certain items of clothes in an emergency. (What if I need to dress up hideously at some point? What if I need to paint the apartment? This shirt would be perfect for that!) When these "emergency" clothes begin to take up more room in my closet than the ones I like and actually wear, then I know it's time for a purging.

Before I even go near my closet, I first set out two boxes and a garbage bag: one box for stuff I can give away to friends, one box for clothes to give to charity, and the garbage bag for clothes that aren't in good enough shape for anyone. Then I go through the piles and ask myself a series of questions:

1. Have I worn this within the last six months? If it's a yes, then I keep it. If it's a no, I keep going.

2. Does this still fit me? If no, and there is no sentimental value, then it goes into whichever box I see fit. If sentimental value applies, I skip to the next question.

3. Why do I still want this? If I can't think of any reason at all, then there's no problem—out it goes. If it could be used for a costume, then it gets relocated to a costume box I keep on the floor of the guest-room closet. It is most difficult to decide what to do if it's for sentimental reasons. If it was a gift and I just feel bad throwing it out, I make myself do it anyway. If it truly does represent something important and memorable, I'll either box it up with my sentimental objects (toys, etc.) or tack it up on my wall for display.

Once it's in a reasonable state again, my closet becomes a well-functioning addition to my room, and all the difficult choices that went into organizing it seem worthwhile.

• **Avoid "miscellaneous."** Each drawer, section of a shelf, or cubby should hold one specific category of items. If you do have to divide a drawer, make sure the combination is logical and clearly defined. For example, if socks and underwear must coexist in a single drawer, use a divider to keep them from getting mixed up. The worst thing you can do is label a drawer "miscellaneous." It always starts innocently enough—some extra baseball cards and homeless photographs—but eventually it mutates into a drawer full of nail clippers, bubblegum wrappers, half-written postcards, and third-grade party invitations. Miscellaneous is the easiest category to put things into and the most impossible to find anything in.

• **Use logical sequencing.** Position what you consider to be similar groups of items near one another. On your bookshelf, for example, you might place your *Harry Potter, My Father's Dragon,* and *Nancy Drew* books on neighboring shelves because they are all series books.

• **Size it up.** Match the size of items to the size of home. Use shallow drawers for small items such as jewelry, belts, socks, and underwear. Use deep drawers for anything that takes up a lot of room, like folded sweaters, sweatshirts, or blankets.

• **Guarantee easy retrieval.** Avoid overstuffing drawers or stacking things on shelves that are too high to reach. Reserve high storage areas for things you don't need regular access to, such as decorations, out-of-season clothes, or books you have already read but want to save.

• **Keep safety in mind.** Don't store anything that is heavy or fragile in too high a place. Ask someone to secure tall bookcases to the wall to avoid toppling. Don't place videos, audiocassettes, or CDs too close to a heat source. If you put TVs, VCRs, and stereos inside a closed cabinet, make sure the unit has plenty of ventilation.

• If you have two dressers, consider using one for items worn all year long (socks, underwear, workout wear, etc.) and the other for seasonal wear (sweaters, pants, T-shirts, shorts) that get switched when the weather changes. Another option: use one dresser for school clothes, the other for weekend wear.

Step 4: Containerize

Finally, you are able to assess exactly what sorts of containers will work best for keeping your categories separate and orderly.

Start by making a list of all the containers you'll need, whether you are planning to gather your containers from around the house or buy them elsewhere. Indicate what you're planning to store inside every item on the list; that way, if you don't find exactly what you are looking for, you can find a creative alternative.

To ensure that you buy the right-sized container, there's one rule to follow: measure, measure, measure *before* you go shopping. There is nothing more irritating than discovering the dividers you just bought are a quarter of an inch too tall for the drawer, or that the bins you found stick too far out over the edge of your shelves.

Remember to bring your tape measure with you on your shopping excursion. You can't be too careful—measure the actual containers to make sure you've got a perfect fit.

Ten Terrific Bedroom Containers

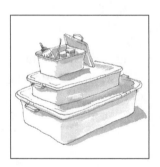

Small, medium, and large plastic containers—great for storing art and scrapbook supplies, extra school supplies, off-season clothes, etc.

Stacking-drawer chest—perfect for use as a bedside table or for storing videos, grooming supplies, or in the bottom of a closet as a small dresser.

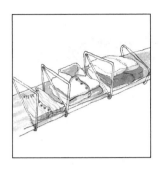

Wire-coated shelf dividers—slides onto closet shelf, ideal for keeping stacks of T-shirts, sweaters, and jeans separated.

Hampers or laundry baskets—great for dry cleaning, laundry, or gym clothes.

Small-parts sorters—useful for storing collections such as coins, jewelry, stamps, shells, etc.

Bookends—ideal for keeping books upright and accessible on shelves.

Magazine holders—placed on bookshelves; perfect for storing collections of magazines or comic books upright.

Shoe racks and bags—good for storing shoes neatly on the floor, wall, or door.

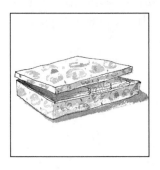

Underbed bins (with or without rollers)—ideal for underbed storage; permit fast, easy retrieval.

Orange or milk crates—stacked on their sides, useful for creating bookshelves, end tables, even storage for socks, underwear, and exercise clothes.

Creative Container Solutions

Make sure your containers are strong enough to withstand repeated use. Consider how much they'll weigh when full and how easy they will be to handle. Also, be creative about using existing storage in nontraditional ways. For example:

- Use a dresser drawer to hold papers, projects, or hobby supplies.
- Use a bookcase to display collectibles, like snow globes, figurines, or model airplanes.
- Adjust shelves so there is no wasted space between them; this will give you room to add an additional shelf or two.
- Out of floor space? Mount the TV and VCR on the wall.
- Unused hangers take up a significant amount of rod space. Remove them and place them in a basket on the floor for convenience.
- Attach hooks, shelves, sorters, and rods to your closet walls and doors to create storage space you never knew you had.

Labeling

Now that you are happy and secure in the knowledge that you've got all your treasures stowed safely in the proper containers, it's time to start labeling. Labels take the remembering out of your system, freeing your mind to concentrate on more important things. Labeling also makes both cleanup and retrieval quick, painless, and mindless activities.

You don't have to label everything on the outside. Find a middle ground where your reminders are plentiful enough to help you stick to your system, but don't detract from the decor of your room.

White labels with bold, black lettering are the standard. But you can get creative with your labels, too. You can write them by hand, use a label maker, or do them on your computer. Cartoons, color-coded pieces of fabric, and newspaper clippings can also do the trick. Size and location are up to your discretion. You may want the labels in your closet to be large and the ones visible in your actual room more subtle. Whichever method you choose, however, one thing is critical: your labels must be legible, attractive, and sticky enough to adhere to the container. No one, not even you, will make sense of your system if the labels look like chicken scratch or if they fall off.

Special Circumstances:
NO CLOSET?

No closet? Don't worry, you aren't the first. Here are some ways to make do without a closet.

Hanging clothes (such as coats, cotton shirts, suits, dresses) can be hung from:

- A tension bar placed between a bookcase and a wall
- Freestanding garment racks
- A clothes tree
- Hooks installed on the wall
- A back-of-door hook
- An armoire or standing closet

Folded clothes can be stored in:

- Dressers
- Underbed bins on wheels
- Bedside table with drawers
- Shelves
- Orange or milk crates stacked in a pyramid

STOP Ask your parents for permission to turn an infrequently used guest room or extra space in the basement into your personal dressing area. Leave a little closet space and a drawer empty for guest, then move all your stuff in there. The key is to try to store all your clothes in one place to avoid running back and forth between rooms to get dressed.

Take polaroids of dress shoes that you keep in boxes on your top shelf, and stick a photo on each box. When you're looking for shoes to go with your dress/outfit, you won't end up forgetting about a pair that would have made a great match and you won't have to rummage through every box to find the ones you need.

Step 5: Equalize

First, give yourself a big pat on the back. You've completely organized your bedroom so that everything you need is attractively and conveniently stored. To keep it that way, make sure you implement the following maintenance program.

1. **Daily touch-ups.** A well-organized bedroom should take no more than ten minutes to straighten up—no matter how messy it gets in the course of a day or evening.

2. **Seasonal tune-ups.** You will inevitably collect more accessories, books, tapes, and interests as the months go by. Once a year, devote an afternoon to sorting through your possessions, old and new. This annual tune-up is a day to look forward to. It's a wonderful time to retreat into your room, discover things that may not be as important as they were a year ago, decide if you want to save a few for memory's sake, and let the rest go. After all, you'll soon be replacing and adding to them with new activities, interests, and passions. Don't forget, as we grow and change, so do our things.

5

School Stuff

Project Checklist	

MATERIALS	Large, strong trash bags
	1 large banker's box labeled "school archive"
	Plain manila file folders
	Organizing containers: file drawers or
	    portable file boxes, binders, notebooks,
	    locker accessories—to be selected later
	Label maker or blank labels and marker

ESTIMATED TIME	School papers 2–3 hours Locker 30 minutes–1 hour Backpack 30 minutes–1 hour

You spend most of your early school years with absolutely no need for a sophisticated organizing system. Elementary school just isn't that demanding.

Then, in junior high, the pace picks up and there's an outpouring of paper and books that only gets heavier as the years progress. Without a reliable and useful system for your home-study area, locker, and backpack, it's virtually impossible to keep track of all the papers and homework assignments that pass through a typical student's hands in an average week. A great deal of important materials can slip through the cracks or end up as Fido's dinner.

Welcome to the world of filing. This section will show you how to transform your collection of loose papers and bursting binders to create a system that's tailor-made to your specific needs. It will also help you determine the best way to set up your locker for a true one-minute pit stop between classes and how to take your overstuffed, backbreaker of a backpack and turn it into a lean, mean transport machine.

A Mountain of Papers

To give you an idea of how fast school papers can pile up, here's a sample breakdown of a typical teen's semester accumulation.

- 5–10 English papers (50–80 pages)
- 1–2 history papers (10–20 pages)
- 40 pages of homework assignments
- 10 take-home quizzes (20–30 pages)
- 100–150 pages of class notes
- 20 readings (10–15 pages)

Total Page Count: 420–620 per semester

PHASE 1: ANALYZE

Answer the following questions as completely and honestly as you can to begin your quest to control your school stuff before it gets control of you.

Question #1: What's Working and What's Not?

 💬 "All my notebooks are color-coded by subject so I can quickly grab the right one even when I'm in a rush."
                                        —Jessica T., 16, Pennsylvania

💬 "I never have any trouble finding my textbooks in my locker because they're all neatly stacked at the bottom."
                                        —Oran K., 14, Illinois

 💬 "I don't know what to keep and what to toss. I end up with so much stuff I can't find anything. The worst thing is that once I lose something, I completely forget about it until the teacher asks for it in class, and by then it's too late."   —Danielle K., 16, California

💬 "I have so much junk in my locker, it often makes me late for class. A book could be right under my nose, but I won't even see it because of all the garbage."
                                        —Amy F., 15, Virginia

💬 "My homework is always getting torn and crushed in my backpack. I get a lot of complaints from teachers."
                                        —Vlad G., 15, Arizona

Put a plus (+) next to what's working and a minus (−) next to what's not.

(+) (−)		(+) (−)	
_____	Desk at home	_____	Papers
_____	Locker	_____	Notes and permission slips
_____	Backpack	_____	Research materials
_____	Notebooks and binders	_____	School supplies
_____	Textbooks	_____	After-school activity gear

More what's working:

_____

_____

More what's *not* working:

_____

_____

Question #2: What's Your Essential 7?

It's time to decide what your Essential 7 is for your home study-area, your backpack, and your locker. Your essential items are those that help you study, track information, and perform your best at school. What could you absolutely not live without? Some teens couldn't imagine life without their computer, while others wouldn't feel complete without their trusty Wite-Out or school binders. These teens have pinpointed their Essential 7. Can you do the same?

Home-Study Area/Paperwork Essentials

Deny F., 17, Michigan	Adi B., 15, Alabama
1. Computer/printer	1. CD player
2. French translater	2. Chemistry books
3. Calculator	3. Pens/#2 pencils
4. Binders	4. Class notes
5. Colored pencils	5. Organizer
6. Textbooks	6. Floppy disks
7. Loose-leaf paper	7. Dictionary

Backpack Essentials

Guy H., 17, New York	Maayan M., 18, Minnesota
1. Novel	1. Bottled water
2. City map	2. Wallet
3. Lunch money	3. Journal
4. MetroCard	4. Notebooks
5. Gameboy	5. House keys
6. Class notes	6. Lip gloss
7. Cell phone	7. Library card

Locker Essentials

John H., 14, Oregon	Erica L., 18, Ohio
1. Spare loose-leaf paper	1. Calculus books
2. Books	2. Sweater
3. Pens/pencils	3. Calculator
4. Notebooks	4. Lip gloss
5. Pictures	5. Organizer
6. Air freshener	6. Locker shelf
7. Floss	7. Mirror

Question #3: What's the Payoff?

Getting a handle on all those piles of crumpled paper, unmarked homework, books, and school supplies isn't easy. Before you dive in, ask yourself what it is you're hoping to get out of it. Is it to get better grades, to save time searching for lost objects, to have more time to socialize with friends? Identify the reason now so you can stay motivated while you organize.

> "To stop freaking out when I can't find my stuff between classes."   —Shachar K., 13, Massachusetts

> "To stop getting low grades on late homework assignments."   —Marcy Y., 17, Iowa

> "To make it to class on time."
>   — Jasmin R., 14, Pennsylvania

> "I want to get into Princeton."   —Zack A., 16, New York

Question #4: What's the Problem?

To get to the heart of your struggle to manage your school stuff, you need to identify what's causing the problems. Check the boxes next to the combination of causes that are getting in your way.

❏ Homeless items	❏ "Out of sight, out of mind" mentality	❏ Sentimental attachments
❏ Inconvenient storage	❏ More stuff than space	❏ Fear of losing creativity
❏ Overly complex system	❏ Disorganized family	❏ Unclear goals and priorities
	❏ "Organizing is boring" mind-set	

Jessi Says

Birth of an Organizing System

When I started junior high school, I had a teacher who was completely disorganized. He assigned homework and projects to no end and was constantly losing the students' work. Often, someone's final grade would leave them scratching their head because it did not amount to the work they had done in class.

When this happened to me, I went right to him to challenge the grade I was given. He told me I would need to prove that I deserved better and requested copies of all my work. At that point, I did not have much of a system for my school stuff. I had saved some work and tossed some, without any real thought. I was unable to prove my point and got stuck with a bad grade on my transcript as a result.

That's when I decided I had to pull it together. I could not let a teacher's mistake ruin my college transcript. Even though my mom had been suggesting filing systems for years, I hadn't been motivated to follow through. This time, I was doing it for myself. (Read about my system in the "Containerize" section later in this chapter.)

PHASE 2: STRATEGIZE

Map Out a Plan!

Now, how do you take the kindergarten model of organization (see Chapter 2) and apply it to your school stuff? Put pen to paper and let the designing begin!

✍ Julie's Work Journal:

Eric's Story

Eric was a ninth-grader drowning in a sea of papers. He often forgot where he wrote down homework assignments, lost research he'd printed off the Internet, left his homework at home instead of handing it in, and found working at his desk impossible because it was always covered with huge, messy stacks of papers and books. He kept trying to set up an organizing system, but nothing seemed to work—or last.

Eric's failure to set up an effective system was caused by three obstacles: (1) an overly complex system; (2) an out-of-sight, out-of-mind mind-set; and (3) fear of losing his creativity.

The complicated systems Eric set up made it almost impossible to remember where to put or find anything. For each class he had about six to ten folders, subdivided into such topics as schedule, class trips, work he liked and might refer to again, work he was unhappy with, interesting handouts, boring handouts, research, etc.

Adding to the confusion was a series of six active folders on his desktop: "urgent," "important," and "semi-important," one each for school and non-school projects. There were so many places for any one piece of paper to go, he never knew where to look. This complex web led him to pile up all his important papers on his desk for fear of losing them in his crazy, mixed-up system.

Finally, as frustrated as Eric was with his mess, he was afraid that the structure and regularity of an organizing system would make him just like everybody else. Eric was a highly creative person, an artist and musician who loved spontaneity.

Our solution for Eric was to create a much simpler filing system, one that would support an easy flow of information and materials between his backpack, locker, and desk area at home. In his home study-area, we separated current papers from old work. We reduced his files to three folders per class—"Current Projects," "Graded Work," and "Class Notes and Handouts."

We eliminated his desktop files altogether. He wrote reminders in his planner as to what projects were due so he wouldn't forget what to work on when. (See Chapter 7 for information on how to choose a planner.) He also made rules about what he would store in his backpack and his locker.

In the end, Eric discovered that getting organized did not take away his charm. In fact, it gave him more time to be spontaneous because he spent less time worrying about and searching for his schoolwork.

Task #1: Define Your Zones

What are the main activities you do in the places where your school stuff goes? There are usually three primary areas for your school stuff: home-study area, backpack, and locker. Define the specific function of each area and determine how to make them work together.

Home-study area—Your desk at home is probably where you do most of your homework. It needs to be equipped with all the supplies you need for studying, big projects, and research, and a good filing system for past work. The main zones of your home-study area might be:

> Study Zone
> Reference Zone
> Filing Zone
> Supply Zone

Backpack—The function of a backpack is simple: to help you *transport* your stuff between point A (your study-area at home) and point B (your locker). The problem with backpacks is that people tend to use them as portable lockers. This is not their purpose and only leads to your walking around with a ton of dead weight on your back before the semester is up. The main zones of your backpack could be:

> School Materials
> After-School Gear
> Lunch
> Personal Supplies

Locker—A home away from home, your locker is the only place at school that's strictly yours. While you may want to express yourself by adding some personal touches to your locker, its main purpose is not decorative. Simply put, a locker's function is to minimize the amount of things you have to carry from class to class throughout the day. The main zones of your locker could be:

> School Materials
> After-School Gear
> Lunch
> Personal Supplies
> Display

Task #2: Mix 'n' Match Zone Planner

Now it's time to figure out the actual contents that belong in each area. Obviously, there is some overlap between textbooks and notebooks, school supplies and accessories you store in each of your three main zones. That's why it's particularly important to plan it out to figure out what goes where, what stays put, and what moves from zone to zone.

First, divide a sheet of paper into three columns (see example below). List your three main zones (home-study area, locker, backpack) in the first column, supplies in the second, and storage units in the third. Assign a letter to each zone (A, B, C, etc.). Then, match the letter of the zone with the supplies and storage units that apply.

After you've assigned all your supplies and units a letter(s), highlight supplies from the center column that will MOVE from area to area in RED. Put a BLUE highlighter on items you will own duplicates of—so that each area has its own supply.

Home-Study Area		
Zones	**Supplies**	**Storage Units**
A-Study	**A**-Notebooks/binders	**A**-Desktop
B-Reference	**A**-Textbooks	**A**-Underneath desk
Filing	**A**-Handouts	**A**-Portable file box
Supply	**A**-Homework assignments	**A**-Binders
	A-Homework to hand in	**A,B**-Bookshelf
	A-Computer and printer	Desk drawers
	B-Novels/books	Pencil drawer
	B-Reference books	Top drawer
	Old graded work	**A**-Middle drawer
	Disks and CDs	**B**-Bottom drawer
	Pens and pencils	Pen/pencil holders
	Scissors, glue, tape, etc.	Floor
	Add your own here:	

Locker

Zones	Supplies	Storage Units
A-School materials	**A**-Notebooks/binders	**A**-Bottom shelf
B-Personal supplies	**A**-Textbooks/books	**A**-Plastic drawers
After-school gear	**A**-Handouts	**B**-Top shelf
Lunch	**B**-Spare clothes	**B**-Coat hook 1
Decorations	**B**-Makeup	**B**-Inside door
	B-Grooming supplies	Coat hook 2
	B-Mirror	
	Pens and pencils	
	Scissors, glue, tape, etc.	
	Floppy disks	
	Spare paper	
	Lunch	
	Sports uniform	
	Dance clothes	
	Add your own here:	

Backpack

Zones	Supplies	Storage Units
A-School materials	**A**-Notebooks/binders	**A**-Main compartment
B-After-school gear	**A**-Books	Front pocket
Lunch	**A**-Homework assignments	**A**-Left side pocket
Personal supplies	**A**-Homework to hand in	Right side pocket
	A-Old graded work	**A**-Plastic folder
	Scissors, tape, glue, etc.	**B**-Travel sacks
	Lunch	
	B-Water bottle	
	B-Sports uniform	
	B-Dance clothes	
	Add your own here:	

💬 "I finally decided to buy two copies of the textbooks that I need—to keep one at home (for reading/studying) *and* one in my locker (for following along in class). It's expensive but saves my parents money in back-injury bills from the doctor!"   —Jim V., 15, Ohio

Task #3: Plan Your Layout

On another piece of paper, draw your desk/study area, locker, and backpack so you can map out what will live where. Use the following illustrations to give some ideas of how you can create zones in each area.

Before

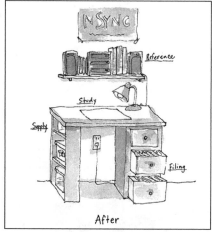

After

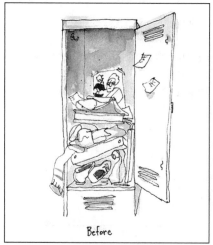

Before

After

Before

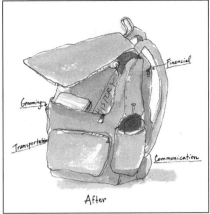

After

💡 Quick Fixes for Zoning Dilemmas in Your Locker

The good news about lockers is that they're so small you can't possibly be a pack rat; the bad news is that they are so small it can be hard to find enough space to create separate zones. Here are some ideas for stretching space:

• Add an extra magnetic hook or wire shelf to create additional storage space for personal items and school supplies.

• If a class doesn't require that you bring in your textbook, keep it at home to save a lot of valuable locker space.

• Store travel-size versions of essentials like hand cream and hair spray in your locker, and leave the larger sizes at home.

Fast Fixes for Zoning Dilemmas in Home-Study Area

Some teens study in their rooms, others in the living room, dining room, or kitchen. Wherever you study, it's essential to keep all your school stuff conveniently stored in the place where you work. Make sure your home-study area includes at least four zones: Study Zone (requires work surface and computer), Reference Zone (for books), Supplies Zone, and Files Zone (for old work you want to save and refer back to).

• Free up work surface on a small desktop by mounting your computer monitor on a swing arm and placing the CPU under your desk

• To give you a bigger work surface, clear your desk of all trinkets and decor. While you are at it, get rid of that huge pencil cup with two hundred pencils and pens, most of which don't work. Keep only as many pencils and pens as you really need. Store infrequently used colored pencils and markers in a container on a shelf.

• If possible, add a shelf above your desk to keep your reference books and materials handy but not cluttering your work surface.

• If you do your homework on the living-room floor or kitchen table, empty a nearby cabinet or end table for storing supplies where you use them. This enables quick and easy cleanup when it's time to eat or have friends over.

• If drawer space is limited, place supplies in small plastic containers with lids and store on nearby shelves or in cabinets. Put files in portable file boxes that can roll under a desk, tuck into a kitchen cabinet, or hide behind the sofa in the living room when not in use.

✍ Julie's Work Journal:
Kathy's Backpack

Kathy had no system in her backpack. School papers, supplies, graded homework, and personal things went in and out in no particular order. She spent a lot of time fishing around in her sack, usually coming up empty with what she was looking for.

Mostly, Kathy's (nonexistent) system made it hard to control the proper flow of stuff in and out of her backpack. Frequently, school papers and permission slips went in without ever coming out. On the other hand, she often made the mistake of removing important items to use at home, such as her wallet, keys, or calculator, then forgetting to put them back in before leaving for school the next day. You can imagine the joy that caused.

To solve the problem, we divided her backpack into two zones: Permanent Items (things that would live in her bag and never be removed) and Transient Items (things that she took in and out every day). To help keep her on track, we inventoried each list of items on either side of a 3 × 5-inch card and laminated it. This enabled her to review it before leaving for school in the morning and leaving for home at the end of the day. Here's what her zones ended up including.

Permanent Items (side pockets)

1. Wallet
2. Keys
3. Graphing calculator
4. Planner
5. Personal items
6. Extra pens/pencils

Transient Items (main compartment)

1. Notebooks
2. Textbooks
3. Homework to hand in
4. Graded work to take home
5. Notes and permission slips
6. After-school activity supplies
7. Lunch

STEP 1: SORT

Sorting will give you the clarity you need to identify what your current priorities are. As always, start by making several piles. Don't worry too much if you come across things you might have overlooked due to a disorganized past, like old papers you want to save or research material you meant to read. This is the time to focus on the present and the future.

Sorting School Papers

Here are some ways you can sort your various school papers by category. Use the following diagram as a model to map out your own sorting system on a separate sheet of paper.

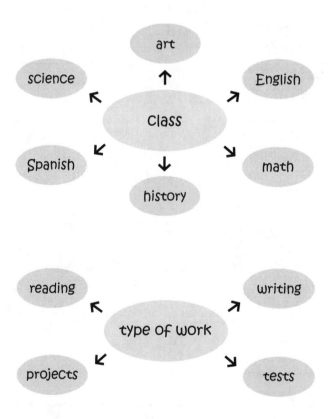

Sorting Your Locker

Here are some ways you can sort the items in your locker. Divide your clothes, books, and supplies into the following categories. Then, use the diagram below to map out your own categories on a separate piece of paper.

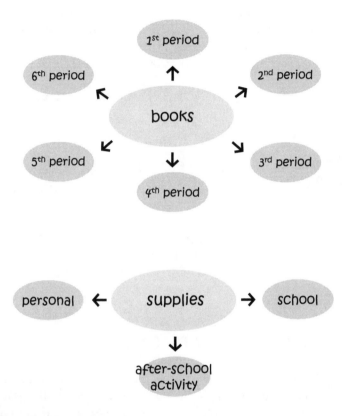

Sorting Your Backpack

Backpacks force you to be as selective as possible because you simply don't have the space to carry around more than your bare necessities. Here are some ways you can sort what stays in the backpack. Once you select your individual sorting method, map out your plan using the diagram below.

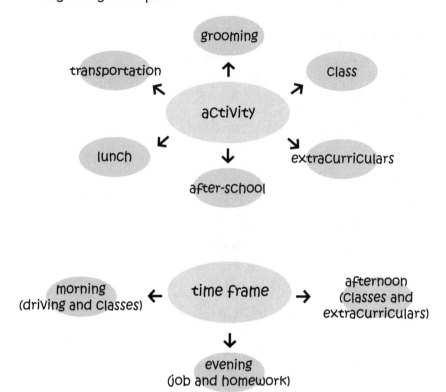

The Ellie System for Organization

Jessi's good friend Ellie developed a system for organizing her school stuff that she has used throughout high school. She's sure it has saved her from the typical back problems that plague many teenagers. It's different from Jessi's system and works extremely well, providing an excellent example of how each person can develop a system that works. This is the Ellie System:

Ellie keeps all her class notes in a one-and-a-half-inch binder. She also has a big three-inch binder that she keeps at home. After every test, she empties out class notes from the small binder to the big binder. The only notes that stay in the one-and-a-half-inch binder are those that she needs for the current chapter of each subject.

Since she takes only the small binder to school, she's not hurting her back by carrying tons of binders around. If she needs to refer to past notes for a final exam, she can always go to the big binder.

Creating a School Archive

Are you holding on to papers from elementary school purely for sentimental reasons? Store only current books, textbooks, supplies, and finished work at your desk area. Place archived work from previous years in a "School Archive" box.

1. Fill a banker's box with thirteen folders, labeled "Kindergarten" through "Twelfth Grade."
2. Sort through the old stuff by year and file it into its proper folder. If you run out of room in the folders don't add new ones—just weed them down further, keeping only the best samples of your work.
3. Store your school archive on the top shelf of your closet, in the attic, or in a spare room. It'll be fun to go throughm it when you're older with kids of your own.

STEP 2: PURGE

Purging Your Papers

Holding on to papers you don't need makes it really difficult to find the ones you need *now*.

You can control the volume of paper in your life by saving only those materials you actually use currently or will definitely need in the near future. Create rules for yourself about what is important and what's not based on how often you actually refer back to things. To decide between the keepers and the losers, ask yourself these

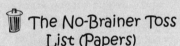 The No-Brainer Toss List (Papers)

- Old calendars and schedules
- Handouts from past classes that you are no longer interested in
- Notes and notebooks from past school years
- Dated research material
- Scrap paper from math and science problems
- Early, rejected drafts of essays and papers

Jessi Says

Organizing Rachel

Though I don't parade myself around school as the most organized girl in town, when your mom is somewhat well known and your notebook and locker scream, "This one is organized! Like mother, like daughter!" people notice the lack of chaos. They tease me warmly about my hyperorganization. A girl named Rachel even asked me to help her get organized. I said yes, I'd be more than glad to.

Rachel had the biggest issues with her backpack. It was totally weighed down by papers that she had stuffed in because she had no idea what to do with them. She had been using a single three-sectioned spiral notebook for all five of her classes' notes. This didn't work because when she ran out of space in one section she had to start writing notes from one subject in another subject's section. As we sorted through the loose papers in her backpack we discovered that the majority of them fell into one of three categories: handouts from English or history class, graded work, and random scraps of paper on which she had written assignments.

Rachel told me she preferred to work in spiral notebooks rather than binders. To solve the problems of class notes getting mixed up between subjects, we decided she would switch to a new five-section spiral notebook. Also, she would buy a second, identical notebook so that when she ran out of room in any one section, she wouldn't have to start mixing subjects again. She would use the small pockets in the dividers between sections for science, Spanish, and math handouts because those classes generated very little extra paperwork. To accommodate the large number of handouts she got from English and history classes, she would buy one separate portfolio folder and designate one side for English handouts and the other for history.

To organize the other loose papers, we worked with Rachel's preference of keeping all subjects together. We got her a clear plastic folder with a string-tie enclosure where she kept all her graded work from every class, the most recent in the very front. This worked well for Rachel because her mind worked chronologically. In other words, if she were looking for old homework, she would remember it first by when she did it (e.g., January) rather than by subject (math). Finally, she liked recording all her assignments in list format in one place, so we decided a small assignment pad would work best.

Working out this system took only about forty-five minutes. Rachel is still in great shape and says her teachers have noticed the improvement in her work habits.

questions of each piece of paper. A "yes" means you should keep it, a "no" that you should toss it.

- Is this paper from a current class?
- Can this help me with a current class or project?
- Do I have the time or the need to read this paper?

Don't get bogged down in sorting through ancient papers. Jump-start your cleanup process by boxing up drawers full of papers you haven't looked at in over a year. Mark a date on your calendar—preferably during one of your vacations or the summer—to retrieve the very old stuff and sort through it. By that time you'll have lived with your new system for a while, and it'll be much easier to get rid of the old and useless.

Always date drafts of each essay or paper you write. That way, once it's time to purge your files, you'll know which version is the most recent.

Purging Your Locker

To make room in your locker for items you can't do without, you need to get rid of absolutely everything you don't need to have at school with you. For instance, each Friday remove papers that are already graded and bring them home to store in the appropriate file drawers, saving your locker for your current work only. You should also remove any handouts or readings that accumulated during the week, notes from friends, and any leftover snacks you didn't get to eat.

Purging Your Backpack

This step involves first cleaning out excess items that are not being used,

🗑 The No-Brainer Toss List (Locker)

- Empty bottles and boxes of lotion, nail polish, hair spray, etc.
- Directions and invites to parties from junior-high school
- Novelty magnets you've outgrown
- Stale or spoiled food from lunches past
- "Let's meet at . . ." notes from ex-boyfriends/girl-friends

🗑 The No-Brainer Toss List (Backpack)

- Chewed and broken pencils, inkless pens, dried-out markers
- Scraps of paper with old shopping lists on them
- Empty candy wrappers
- Last year's *Cosmo Girl* magazine
- Old homework (store it at home)
- Permission slips for past school trips you never gave to your parents

then deciding what you will and will not carry to and from school on a daily basis. You want to travel light and comfortably.

STEP 3: ASSIGN A HOME

It's homecoming time for your most important school-related items! Once you know exactly what you are keeping, it's time to decide where you are going to store each item. It's important to trust your system, so consider the following guidelines before diving in.

Assign a Home: Papers

Avoid "miscellaneous." The biggest mistake you can make is to label a folder or file "miscellaneous." When it comes to finding your homework, old papers, or class notes, you'll have an easier time finding your stuff if you assign it a specific location from the very beginning.

Use logical sequencing. It's very important to keep similar groups of items next to one another. When it comes to your home-study area, position computer-related items like floppy disks and your printer next to your computer. The same rule applies to paperwork. Keep all your materials (assignments, homework, research) for each class close together so you can quickly find what you're looking for.

STOP **Keep safety in mind.** Don't place computer equipment, printers, or heavy books on makeshift shelves that were not meant to hold heavy items. If you need to add a shelf, ask for help to ensure that the proper anchors, supports, and screws are used for solid installation. If you need to run wires, check with your parents to be sure you are not overloading circuits.

Assign a Home: Locker

Easy access. Everything in a locker is already within reach, but you can take further steps to enhance that feature—keep your books at the bottom of your locker with your first-period stuff on top, second-period stuff next, and so on. Rotate your books by putting the ones from your last class last in the lineup and picking up the ones that are first in the lineup for your next class.

Use logical sequencing. Keeping your school and personal stuff separate can help you get moving between classes and after school. Your lunch and personal items could live on the top shelf, while your school stuff (binder, notebooks, textbooks) can work well on the lower shelves.

Assign a Home: Backpack

Easy access. There's nothing worse than all your stuff floating around loose in your backpack. Keep items you use often (wallet, house keys, ID) in the front pockets of your backpack for easy retrieval.

Size it up. Think big when it comes to your main backpack compartment. Things like binders, notebooks, folders, and sports uniforms can all work well in this area.

STEP 4: CONTAINERIZE

Six Sensational Containers for Home-Study Area

Here is where you get to add some style, flair, and pizzazz to your filing system. Make good use of the following containers to boost the speed with which you file and retrieve information. This will go a long way toward making sure that yours is a system you enjoy and trust.

Portable file boxes–perfect for paper storage and can be moved in and out of closets, etc.

Three-ring binders—with their many dividers, binders are the ideal place to store loose-leaf papers. Use one-inch binders for those you intend to carry with you, up to three-inch binders that will stay at home.

Stacking plastic drawers—a practical way to add storage for supplies to a desk with no drawers. Place to the side or under desk.

Project box—perfect for creative people who want their projects accessible yet organized on desktop.

Rolling caddy or taboret—excellent for storing school, art, and scrapbook supplies; rolls under a desk when not in use.

Computer cart—fits your computer into a small space. Frees up desk space, too.

Keep two paper trays on top of or next to your desk. One can serve as your "School To-Do" bin (the work that's yet to be completed) and the other as the "Personal To-Do" bin (personal projects such as letters you want to write, research for summer camps, etc.). This way, you can balance your time and visualize exactly how much work you have ahead of you.

Six Sensational Containers for Your Locker

When buying containers for your locker, be very careful with size. Lockers have a funny way of appearing larger than their actual measurements, so measure the dimensions of yours before you purchase anything. Here are some helpful, space-saving containers you might want to consider using in your locker.

Add-a-shelf unit—wire-coated shelf placed on the floor of your locker doubles surface storage for books, papers, after-school supplies.

Stacking plastic drawers—stacking drawers placed on the floor of your locker help you organize and categorize supplies.

Pencil/pen compartment—hangs magnetically on the inside of the locker door to keep writing materials at your fingertips.

Top shelf basket or bin—instead of having to stand on tiptoe to see what you've got in the back of your locker's top shelf, place everything in a plastic bin that you can pull out. If you want, you can use two smaller bins with different colored lids to distinguish between personal items and school/after-school supplies.

Bulletin board—magnetically mounted on the inside of the locker door, this is the perfect place to stick photographs, to-do lists, and important papers.

Magnetic hooks—add additional hanging options to your locker for supplies, lunch, backpack, etc.

Five Fantastic Containers for Your Backpack

If you don't have enough pockets and compartments built into your backpack, you can subdivide the big pocket with smaller sacks and organizers. Here are some ideas for how to containerize your backpack.

Pencil/pen case—to keep your writing materials safe and accessible.

Makeup/personal-care pouches—to keep your essentials orderly and in one, easy-to-locate place.

Portable CD and diskette holders—for organizing and protecting your music and floppy disks.

Wallet—this may sound obvious, but it's hard to find the right wallet. Find something you like with sections for bills, coins, ID, transportation pass to help you keep all your vital documents in one place.

Cord and charger pouch—if you keep your cell-phone charger and or laptop with you, store the chargers and cords neatly in a zippered sack so they don't get tangled up in your bag.

• When buying a new backpack, bring your old backpack filled with all your essentials to the store with you. When you find a backpack you like, actually take your stuff out of your old backpack and test how it fits into the new candidate.

• Look for a backpack with a lot of compartments to help create separate zones. And make sure it's made of sturdy material, with well-padded straps.

• Try on a prospective backpack when filled to make sure it's comfortable.

Jessi Says

Containerizing My Papers

Once I became motivated to organize my school stuff, I sat down to brainstorm about all the different papers I need to keep track of for each class. I came up with four consistent categories: assignments from teachers (worksheets, readings), homework to hand in, graded work returned to me, and regular class notes. These categories became the foundation of my paper flow system, which includes containers at home, in my backpack, and in my locker. Here's what I do.

Every September, I create a separate binder for each class and divide each into four sections labeled as follows: "Assignments," "Class Notes," "Old Work," and "To Hand In." Some classes have special kinds of papers specific to just them. For example, the periodic table of elements was something I needed to draw upon often when I took chemistry, so I made a special section in my chemistry binder for all the reference tables. In Spanish, I made a special section for verbs and vocabulary, organized alphabetically like my own little dictionary.

I keep my binders in my locker. Each class has a different color binder so I can easily grab the one I need when I am in a hurry. When I have homework in any one of the classes, I take just those binders home that night. I keep a portable three-hole punch in my locker and another one at home so I can always put work away immediately—there's no risk of losing anything that way. Last, I keep an extra pack of lined paper in my locker just in case I run out; that way, I never have to mix notes from different classes.

As the year goes on, of course, my binders can get very full and heavy, so I need to lighten the load. Our school year is broken up into quarters, so I have a portable file box at home set up with two corresponding folders for each class for each quarter: "Old Work" and "Class Notes." The folder colors match the colors of the binders so that I never mix anything up. At the end of each quarter I empty out my binders into the appropriate sections.

Though it seems like a lot of work, having to put in a good two hours before school starts each September, I can breeze right through the year without ever having to search for one little past assignment. And if a teacher loses my work (it's been known to happen), I can instantly produce a copy.

Containerizing Extra-Credit: Labeling

Notebooks and folders allow for a lot of creativity with labeling. Since your notebooks and folders need to be read and understood only by you, you can use any type of writing that strikes your fancy, whether it be large, block letters, your own distinctive (but legible and neat!) handwriting, or a computerized printout.

When it comes to labeling drawers, attach the labels to the inside so you don't ruin the exterior surfaces or detract from your room's look.

For backpacks, attach labeled key tags to zippers to indicate the contents. Or place a note in each pocket to identify what goes inside.

Silly as it may seem at first, physically labeling the various zones of your locker can make all the difference in the world—especially when you first set up your system. Visual reminders of where things belong will go a long way to speeding up your pit stops between classes.

STEP 5: EQUALIZE

Good for you! All your school stuff is finally organized in a way you can understand. Here's how to stay on top of the situation:

Daily Touch-Ups

• Set aside two to three minutes at the end of each day to close up your locker and make sure it's ready for your arrival at school the next morning.

• Take two to three minutes at the end of each day to review the contents of your backpack and get rid of anything that's not necessary.

• Set aside ten minutes at the end of each day, when you're through with your homework, to sort, file, and purge new and older papers.

Seasonal Tune-Ups

• Maintenance is a top priority when it comes to school papers because classes, activities, projects, and responsibilities change frequently. Take a few hours at the beginning of every semester to update your system and keep up to date with your new schedule.

• Use the beginning of each semester as a time to clean house, to give the contents of your locker a thorough inspection, and to make sure that you're not unwittingly holding on to any unnecessary items.

• Set aside fifteen minutes or so every four weeks to take home anything you don't need at school and to throw out anything you don't need in general.

• Check your backpack's containers. Are there makeup or grooming products that you haven't used in the last month? Are there CDs you haven't listened to more than once or twice? This is the time to decide which items have worn out their welcome and to pare down your essentials.

• At the beginning of each year, decide if you are going to get a new backpack. Make sure it includes the features from the current one you have enjoyed and the additional features you felt were missing.

6

Photos, Memorabilia, Collections

Project Checklist	
MATERIALS	Trash bags 2 medium-size boxes labeled "give away" and "needs repair" Organizing supplies: shoe boxes, photo albums, collection boxes, display shelves, etc.—to be selected later Dust cloth
ESTIMATED TIME	Photos 6–8 hours Memorabilia 3–5 hours Collections 1–3 hours

Your teenage years are a time of change and discovery. New interests take the place of old ones, new schools bring new friends and new hobbies, new experiences forge new opinions. By the end of this six- to seven-year period, you can hardly remember who you were when you last ate off the kids' menu.

Fortunately, you have your photographs, memorabilia (special mementos, souvenirs, keepsakes), and collections to help you capture and hold on to the memories and experiences of your childhood. A great source of reassurance during the turbulent teens, these touchstones can inspire confidence and reinforce identity. It's not realistic to expect that you can give them up as easily as you would an old pair of shoes.

The challenge with things like collections and memorabilia is that unless you devote a lot of time to keeping them updated and organized, they can multiply and take over your space. For example, if you collect stuffed animals and don't keep them in order, you might end up swimming in a sea of fluffy, furry bunnies. They can become clutter instead of treasures.

This chapter is devoted to helping you devise an organizational system for these keepsakes so you can preserve, enjoy, and carry your childhood with you as you move into adulthood. You'll learn to distinguish between items from your past that you can live without—and those you can't. You'll decide which items to display and which to store in a closet, attic, or basement. You'll also learn how to store your old favorites in a way that will still allow you to enjoy them.

PHASE 1: ANALYZE

Let me guess: The only reason that pile of old camp photos and letters has been in that same corner for the last year is that you've been meaning to mount them all in an album but just haven't gotten around to it yet. Let me guess again: The same goes for the foreign coins strewn around your desk collecting dust. The truth is, these sorts of weekend projects always seem to fall to the bottom of your to-do list. The trick is to tackle them head on. By answering the next four questions, you will be on your way to doing just that.

Question #1: Working and What's Not?

 "I collect scraps of fabric for sewing and craft projects. I keep solid colors in one basket and printed fabrics in another." —Mira S., 14, Pennsylvania

"I collect pennies, and this might sound odd . . . mango seeds. The pennies are all in a huge glass jar on my dresser, and the dried mango seeds are lined up on one shelf." —Josiane L., 14, Massachusetts

 "I've collected photos and postcards from around the world. But they are sitting in a big drawer—I wish there were some way to display them better." —Kelly M., 17, South Carolina

💬 "I collect photos, playbills, postcards, Ty Beanie Babies, and stuffed animals. I think I have too many collections or something, because I don't know where one ends and another begins."—Christina P., 14, New York

Put a plus (+) next to what's working and a minus (−) next to what's not.

(+) (−)	(+) (−)
_____ Old school papers	_____ CD collection
_____ Photos	_____ Stuffed-animal collection
_____ Photo albums	_____ Sports-card collection
_____ Scrapbooks	_____ Souvenirs
_____ Posters	_____ Old birthday cards
_____ Display items (frames, trophies, etc.)	_____ School memorabilia
More what's working:	More what's *not* working:
_____	_____
_____	_____
_____	_____

Question #2: What's Essential?

Next on our agenda: finding out what really matters to you. Ask yourself what you couldn't live without. Between your vacation photos, snow globe collection, and baseball cards, what is your absolute favorite? Here are some examples from other teens to help you get started (a hint: sometimes—not always—the quantity will be a tip-off).

Photo Memorabilia Collection Essentials	
Sean P., 12, Michigan	Jonathan L., 15, West Virginia
Favorite collection: Pokemon cards Number of cards: 500	Favorite collection: baseball cards Number of cards: 300

Elizabeth D., 14, Missouri	Bob C., 16, Texas

Favorite memorabilia: photos
Number of photo boxes and
   photo albums: 14
	Favorite collection: Dallas Cowboys
	   memorabilia
	Number of items: 40

Cecily N., 13, Indiana	Shawna P., 14, New Jersey
Favorite collection: Beanie Buddies Number collected: 42	Favorite memorabilia: childhood books Number of books: 250

Question #3: What's the Payoff?

Every teen has a different reason for wanting to organize this part of his or her life. For some, it's primarily practical: your stuff is literally taking over your space. For others, it's about making the transition out of childhood—suddenly your stuffed teddy bears embarrass you when certain friends visit. Whatever the reason, it's important to articulate clearly before wading through the clutter, and use it to motivate yourself as you work toward your goal.

💬 "I recently transferred to a new school. I need a way to organize the photos of friends from my old neighborhood so I don't forget them."   —Jessica Y., 16, Hawaii

💬 "I need an organized and itemized list of everything in my collection for trading and selling." —Mike G.-W., 15, Texas

💬 "I saved the ticket stubs to every Yankee game I've gone to. I need a place to organize this collection so I can share it with friends."   —Emily D., 16, New York

💬 "I'm tired of spending entire Sundays looking through piles of photos just to find a particular picture. I want to have more access to my memories."

—Liba R., 14, Connecticut

Question #4: What's the Problem?

There are many potential obstacles to a pruned-down, well-organized, and well-displayed selection of your favorite keepsakes. The key is to identify what exactly is holding you back, then tackle those obstacles one by one. Check the boxes next to those problems that may be affecting you. Refer back to Chapter 1 for an explanation of each.

❏ Homeless items
❏ Inconvenient storage
❏ Overly complex system

❏ "Out of sight, out of mind" mentality
❏ More stuff than space
❏ Disorganized family
❏ "Organizing is boring" mind-set

❏ Sentimental attachments
❏ Fear of losing creativity
❏ Unclear goals and priorities

✍ Julie's Work Journal:

Molly's Story

Molly's room was littered with more than 250 stuffed animals. They were all over the place—on her bed, on the floor, tucked into her bookshelves. Some were even under her bed and in her closet. This was a collection that began the day she was born. At age fifteen, she was not ready to give up any of them—but they had taken over.

There were three problems causing the mess: the collection had no home, Molly had many more animals than would fit on the surfaces in her room, and she was sentimentally attached to each one. There was nothing wrong with keeping this collection, but it needed to be organized.

We purchased six stuffed-animal "hammocks" from a catalog—triangular pieces of mesh netting that could be mounted with simple hooks in the corner of any wall. We hung three in the corner to the left of her bed and three in the corner to the right. The result was that Molly could keep all the stuffed animals, and they were proudly displayed on the wall, off the floor, as a decorative display framing her bed.

PHASE 2: STRATEGIZE

 Map Out a Plan!

You've thought about what's most important to you, what's working, and what isn't. Finally, you're ready to begin mapping out a plan for all your photos, collections, and memorabilia.

Task #1: Define Your Zones

In this case, zones really mean categories. Here's where you begin thinking about the different groups that your photos, collections, and memorabilia fall into. How will you organize all the keepsakes that have accumulated over the years?

The following are examples of possible zones you may want to adopt to when rearranging your:

- Photos Zone (camera, film, negatives, family photos, friend photos, etc.)
- Jewelry Collection Zone (earrings, bracelets, beads, rings, necklaces, etc.)
- Childhood Memories Zone (children's books, clothes, drawings, etc.)
- Stuffed-Animal Collection Zone (bears, dolls, Beanie Babies, bunnies, etc.)
- Vacation Mementos Zone (photos, airplane tickets, brochures, T-shirts, etc.)

Task #2: Mix 'n' Match Zone Planner

Once you've mapped out your zones, you're all ready to start mixing and matching. List your zones in the first column, supplies in the second, and your storage units in the third. Label each zone with a letter (A, B, C, etc.), then assign each item in columns two and three the letter or letters of the zone(s) to which it relates. For example, if you keep your theater stuff "B" in a box underneath the bed, place the letter "B" by the items "ticket stubs," "playbills," and "autographs" in the second column and again by "scrapbook" and "under the bed" in the third column.

Zones	Supplies	Storage Units
A-Photos	**A**-Film	**A**-Shoe boxes
B-Theater Stuff	**A**-Rolls of blank film	**A**-Memory box
Baseball Card Collection	**A**-Pictures	**A**-Photo albums
Jewelry Collection	**A**-Camera	**A**-Glass frames
Stuffed-Animal Collection	**A**-Negatives	**B**-Under the bed
Childhood Memories	**B**-Ticket stubs	**B**-Scrapbook
Vacation Mementos	**B**-Playbills	Backpack/handbag
	B-Autographs	Desk drawer
	Baby clothes	Entertainment center
	Brochures	Bookshelves
	Coins	Jewelry box
	Earrings	Mounted wall-shelves
	Bracelets	*Add your own here:*
	Add your own here:	

 Creating Space for Photos

- Designate a shelf in your closet, a drawer in one of your dressers or your desk, or cabinet shelves for storing your camera equipment, film, and album supplies. This way you'll never lose that Kodak moment.

PHASE 3: ATTACK

STEP 1: SORT

Here comes the fun part. Time to sort through the mountains of stuff you've collected over the years. As always, the plan of attack is to start by gathering all your photos, collections, and memorabilia from every corner they may be hiding in. Once you've gathered all your items, you should be able to tell exactly how big a job this will be. Now dive in and start sorting!

Sorting Your Photos
Here are some categories that work well for subdividing photos.

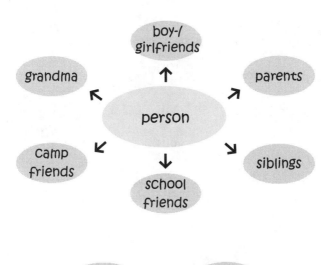

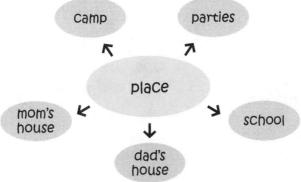

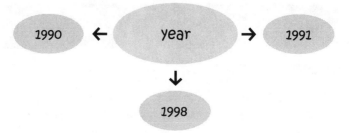

Sorting Your Memorabilia

Be creative. The possibilities here are endless.

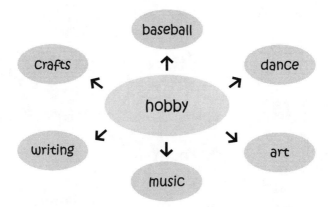

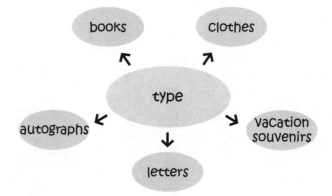

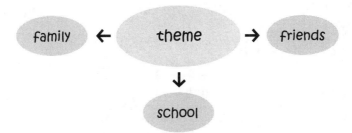

Sorting Your Collections

Here are some ways you can sort your collections.

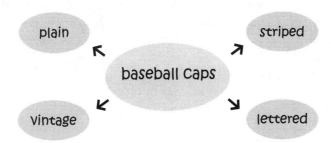

Or you can sort:
- Chronologically by age of item
- Chronologically by when the item came into your possession
- By monetary value from most to least valuable
- By monetary value from least to most valuable
- By size, placing items like toy cars and dolls on display areas in order of size
- Alphabetically, organizing books and CDs by the author's and artist's name

STEP 2: PURGE

Ready or not . . . it's time to purge the unnecessary so you can make more room for the real treasures.

Purging Your Photos

Everyone loves looking at photos. But nobody likes to see blurry shots or unflattering pictures of themselves. Simply put, bad photos take all

Jessi Says

My Candle Collection

I've been collecting candles for six years, more or less. I have more than a hundred candles, all displayed on two L-shaped shelves high up in a corner of my room.

The collection started unintentionally when I was ten. I began picking up some candles with nice scents here and there, placing them around my room. My mom noticed this and began bringing me a candle every time she came back from a business trip. I would never burn them because I didn't want to waste them; I was saving them for special occasions, which never actually occurred. I continued to accumulate candles that I liked to look at or smell, until I realized I had so many around my room that it had become a collection.

Once it occurred to me that I had a collection that I didn't have to start from scratch, I decided to continue to add to it. The candles were scattered around my room. I had a shelf built high up in a corner so I could see them and they'd be out of the way. I began looking for candles with interesting shapes: a tea set, a wizard. As the collection continued to grow, I had to add another shelf, on the other side of the corner, making an L-shape. After a couple of years, I needed more room, so I had another L-shape built about eighteen inches above the first.

Since the candles are on display high up, they are organized so that the smallest are in the front of the shelves and the largest are in back. This way I can see all of them. Also, some are organized into little scenarios. For example, I have one candle of a fat jogging lady running toward a candle in the shape of a big cake and another of a cherry pie. I never burn any of my candles; I only want to add to, not destroy, my collection. I like that I can always look at it and admire a different one in a new way. I also have something specific to look for on every trip I go on, and a reliable idea for a gift for my birthday. The collection gives people who visit me something new to look at every time they come over.

the fun out of reminiscing. If you cringe every time you come across your Frankenstein moments, why hang on to them? Moving these pictures to the toss pile will help you control not only the number of photos you keep but the amount of work you have in store for you.

Organizing Digital Photos

If you have a digital camera, you already know the joy of instantly being able to delete photos that didn't turn out well. It sure saves time in getting rid of the excess later on. In the event that you didn't purge as you snapped, now's the time to get rid of the massive number of photos taking up your hard drive.

Begin by setting up folders by category in "My Pictures," according to how you'd like to group your photos—e.g., "Friends—School," "Friends—Camp," "Family," "Vacations," "Pets," "Art."

Open each photo, delete the bad shots, name the photos you are keeping with recognizable titles, and then move them to the appropriate folder. Working one to two hours at a time, you can get a large number of on-line photos under control before you know it. If your photos come from the developer's or your camera on rewritable CDs or disk, be sure to store and label the disks to match your computer system. A computer crash would eliminate all your photos in an instant, so keeping the backup on disk is advisable.

Purging Your Memorabilia

We are firm believers in the importance of saving memorabilia. Letters, trophies, and certain objects can trigger memories that bring us joy and some perspective on who we are. That said, the key is moderation. Be selective and keep only memorabilia that has strong emotional value to you. Then organize what you're keeping so it can be easily accessed and a pleasure to look through.

Purging Your Collections

Purging items from collections past and present can be a difficult task because of the enthusiasm we once had for these items. Still, there's no denying that as a collection grows, there are bound to be certain elements that don't measure up anymore.

The No-Brainer Toss List (Photos)

- Doubles—if a year has passed and no one's asked for them yet.
- Unflattering shots—also known as possible blackmail material. Eyes half closed, goofy smile showing? They're your photos. Why punish yourself?
- Bad shots—anything that's out of focus, too dark, or features a partially severed head. Sure, the shot would've been good if it were clearer, but in a year or two you won't remember who that blurry shape was anyway.

🗑 The No-Brainer Toss List (Memorabilia)

- Ratty, broken toys and games with parts missing
- Old birthday cards with no special message written inside
- The wrapping paper from every gift you were ever given
- Receipt from the hot dog you bought on your class trip to D.C.
- Any object whose reason for saving you no longer can remember

For example, Shari collects nail polish. When she started, she'd collect any nail polish she found that was cheap, colorful, and fun. As her collection expanded, however, she realized she'd ended up with many bottles that were practically the same color, just different brands. Eventually, she decided to weed out the duplicates, triplicates, and quadruplicates, keeping one of each color in only the brands she liked most. She also organized them by color groupings to avoid further duplication and waste.

STEP 3: ASSIGN A HOME

When you are ready to start assigning homes, the main question to ask yourself is whether you want these items on display or in storage. The answer depends on how often you want to be able to "visit" them. If they inspire you on a daily basis, put them on display. If you are short on space and/or prefer to take only periodic trips down memory lane, send them to storage. It can be fun to pull out old photos and memorabilia on a rainy day. Here are some ideas for displaying and storing various items.

Assigning Collections—on Display
- On open bookshelves
- In a special cabinet with glass doors
- On shelves mounted high up on your walls
- On a wall, hung with hooks

Assigning Collections—in Storage
- In boxes under the bed
- In a big chest at the foot of the bed
- Inside a closet on shelves

Assigning Photos—on Display

- On shelves in photo albums
- On tables in photo cubes
- On the wall in photo collages
- On the wall or dresser top in frames

Assigning Photos—in Storage

- On a shelf in shoe boxes
- In cartons in the attic
- In a dresser drawer

- Store your digital camera and video equipment next to your TV or computer for easy access and viewing.

- Designate a special pocket in your backpack for undeveloped film so you don't forget to drop it off at the photo store.

Assigning Memorabilia—on Display

- Tacked to a big bulletin board on the wall
- On open shelving
- Mounted on the wall arranged in cubbies
- On a shelf in scrapbooks

Assigning Memorabilia—in Storage

- In a closet in plastic containers, clearly labeled on the outside
- In the attic (stay away from the garage or basement—too humid!)
- Under the bed in rolling bins
- In a cedar chest at the foot of the bed
- In archival memorabilia boxes

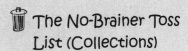

The No-Brainer Toss List (Collections)

- Three of the same easily acquired, common baseball cards
- Stuffed animals that are ripped beyond repair, with the stuffing pouring out
- The gaudy necklace your ex-boyfriend bought that you've never worn since

Giveaways

If you can't bring yourself to throw anything away, consider giving your castoffs to a

- charity (old toys, games, stuffed animals, T-shirts, etc.)
- sibling (CDs you no longer want, dolls, etc.)
- friend's sibling (old toys, remains of sticker collection, etc.)
- library (books for the stacks, magazines for the archives, etc.)

Jessi Says

Jessi's Memory Wall

I'm a pretty sentimental person. When I was around twelve, I needed to make space in my room for the increased volume of school stuff, clothes, and dance gear that came with junior high school. I went through all my old childhood books, clothes, dolls, and games, picked the ones I wanted to keep, and my mom and I put them in a big lidded basket on a high shelf in the guest-room closet. We delivered the rest of the stuff that was in good condition to a shelter for battered women and children. It felt good to share the things I still cared about with other kids who I knew would enjoy playing with them, too. To tell you the truth, doing that made it much easier for me to let those things go.

Even though I stored away the majority of my childhood playthings and books, there is some memorabilia I like to keep visible—reminders of friends, events, performances, and shows that were wonderful, special experiences for me. I started out by taping some photos from my sixth-grade graduation and a few friends on the outside of my closet door. Before long, this double door came to be known as my memory wall . . . I continue to tape, nail, and tack all kinds of special reminders on the doors, collage-style. To date, here's what I've got on my memory wall:

- Ticket stubs to all the Broadway shows and movies I've seen and loved (*Rent, Fosse, Ragtime, De La Guarda, Phantom of the Opera, Urinetown,* and the movie *My Best Friend's Wedding*)
- Photo stamp of me and my best friend Jed taken at FAO Schwarz when we were thirteen
- Identification badge from Hipo.com, a teen website where I interned
- Backstage press pass to the Jingle Ball (which I reviewed for Hipo.com)
- My favorite pair of ripped jeans from seventh grade. Tucked into one pocket are the lyrics to two of my favorite songs. There's a "Go P.S. 29" button pinned on the back and a pearl bracelet I wore for Halloween as a princess in eighth grade in the other back pocket.
- "Best Buddies" card my friend Stephanie gave me when we were twelve.
- Boarding pass for the connection I missed on my way to meet my dad in the Cayman Islands. I got stuck overnight in Florida and had to stay in a hotel all alone. What an experience!

- *Archie* cartoon of sleepy person being woken with "Wakey, wakey, rise and shine"—given to me by a camp counselor who said that every morning, even before she ever saw the cartoon
- Two tambourines from various bar mitzvahs
- Lyrics from "We Are the World," which I had to sing in a show once with a big group, unrehearsed, and the music ended up playing over and over until we had sung the whole song about fifteen times

STEP 4: CONTAINERIZE

Five Fantastic Containers for Photos

Here are some ideas for storing your photos.

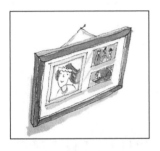

Frames—display and protect your favorite photos. Inexpensive frames made of acrylic, paper, wood, and brass are available in art-supply stores and houseware stores. Some fun frames are made for collages, with different-size openings in which you can arrange a collection of photos.

Albums—preserve and display a large number of important photographs. If you have photos in different sizes, look for binder-style albums that sell various sleeve inserts to accommodate photos of different sizes and orientations.

Shoe boxes—roomy enough to store a great volume of photos, as well as negatives.

Scrapbooks—allow you to creatively display your pictures and accompanying paper memorabilia (invitation to your first wedding reception/communion/bar mitzvah/birthday party and photos from event).

Photo mount squares—two-sided adhesive squares that will enable you to mount photos to scrapbook pages without glue sticks (glue will ruin photos).

Four Phenomenal Containers for Memorabilia

Banker's boxes—great for report cards, old artwork, and schoolwork.

Cedar-lined trunk—protects treasures, including clothing, papers, and objects. Add a sachet of lavender to keep moths out and smell nice.

✒ Julie's Personal Journal:

My Own Childhood Memory Box

One way to save memorabilia is to take a big box or trunk and create a sort of treasure chest. You save only as much as will fit, and as time goes on, you may remove some things to make room for more memories. The size of the container will vary depending on the specific period you're commemorating, the type of person you are, etc. My memories from childhood all fit into a little decorative shoe box. It fits on a shelf with my photo albums, and although there isn't much in there, it's just enough to trigger great memories for me. Here's what's in it.

- Class pictures from third and fourth grade with my two favorite teachers, Mrs. Singer and Mr. Cohen
- Autograph books from my last year two years before moving from my old neighborhood, capturing the names of all my old friends
- Photo album from my overnight camp, Galil, summer of 1972
- Letters from high school and college friends and boyfriends
- A photo of me and my childhood idol Bette Midler, meeting backstage at the *Clams on the Halfshell* review when I was eighteen, plus her autograph
- An autographed *Playbill* from another of my idols, Katharine Hepburn
- Two honor badges I earned as a Girl Scout when I was eight years old
- Autobiography from ninth-grade English class; tells a lot about who I was then (surprising how much is still the same)
- Script and ticket from original high school musical called *The Box* I performed in, playing the chemistry teacher
- Essay I wrote about my dog Happy when he was eleven years old
- Junior high and high school IDs
- Small sculpture I made with wood and nails in fourth grade

Labeling Photos

• Write the names of the people in the photos on the backs, or label them in your album. You'd be surprised how quickly you can forget the names of all the people in your sixth-grade class. With digital photos, add a note indicating who the people are.

• Because albums and scrapbooks are usually stacked, position the labels to the binding as you would with a regular book.

STEP 5: EQUALIZE

Yippee! Pat yourself on the back. All your memories are in order! Here's how to maintain your pride and joy by doing organizational touch-ups.

Daily Touch-Ups

Don't let your new photos pile up. Any time you find yourself with two or more packs lying around, put them in a new photo album, shoe box, or scrapbook . . . or add them to an already existing one.

Memorabilia has a way of piling up, too. Create a box for possible keepers and be tough deciding what makes the grade; more often than not, you have a pretty good sense within a day or two.

Each time you add to your existing collections, take a moment to review the older contents, with an eye to possible purging.

Seasonal Tune-Ups

Summer vacation and school breaks offer the perfect opportunity to go over your stash of photos and papers so you can choose the ones you want to keep, toss, or display. This is a fun activity that you're bound to enjoy. Just leave yourself a realistic amount of time, as reminiscing is part of the fun.

Once a year, sort through your box of potential memorabilia and figure out what you want to add to your memory boxes and scrapbooks and what you want to toss.

Maintaining your collections is a wonderful activity for a rainy day. Every time you find a new collectible, you can rearrange your collection to incorporate it.

Once a year, take some time to review your collections and determine if you've outgrown an old collection or started a new one. If so, make sure it's time to apply the SPACE formula, sorting your new items, purging the old ones, assigning homes, and taking down old displays to make room for the new.

PART 3

Organizing Your Time

7

Tools for Time Management

💬 "I have way too much to do . . . and never enough time!"
—Jennifer G., 16, Michigan

💬 "There's too much pressure. My list of projects and tasks is so overwhelming . . . I procrastinate and end up doing nothing."
—Rob E., 14, Pennsylvania

💬 "My life is so out of balance! Help! How do I fit everything in?"
—Lisa L., 17, California

Between homework, after-school activities, friends, family, and a zillion other events competing for your time, a teen's life can be shockingly full of activity. It's not easy fitting it all in, but you'd be surprised how much you can get done when you learn to organize your time.

Good time management puts you in command of your days and, ultimately, your life. It enables you to stay balanced and feel a satisfying sense of accomplishment every day.

By developing good time-management skills, you can handle more, and celebrate the many things going on in your life, instead of letting them overwhelm you.

In this chapter, you'll learn the three basic tools that will help you manage and balance all the departments of your life. The subsequent chapters on studying, after-school activities, and social life will show you how to combine these tools with the "Analyze, Strategize, and Attack" process to create the life you want.

The Three Basic Tools of Time Management

To get control of your time, you'll need to master these three basic tools:

1. Planner/datebook
2. Time map
3. WADE formula

TOOL #1: THE PLANNER/DATEBOOK

Spreading your to-do lists among a combination of Post-its, McDonald's napkins, notebook paper, and the back of your hand is a recipe for confusion. In order to keep track of the zillions of to-dos, due dates, parties, appointments, and ideas that flow into your life, you need to have a single, consistent planner/datebook. The type you choose (paper, Palm Pilot, datebook, wall calendar) is completely up to you, but without one you will undoubtedly forget important information and spend more time trying to remember what to do next than getting anything done.

The goal is to make your planner the one and only place you record all your information about what to do and where to be. You must be able to rely on it and trust it completely.

Therefore, you must find a planner that is a good match for you. There are so many choices on the market; how does anyone decide? Here are some guidelines to keep in mind before making your selection.

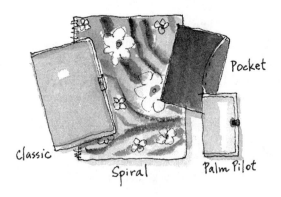

CHOOSING A PLANNER

Choice #1: Paper or Electronic?

Paper

Paper planners work best if you are a visual/tactile person. You fit this category if:
• Your thinking flows easiest when writing things down, pen to paper.
• Physically writing things out helps you remember them better.
• You tend to remember where on a page you wrote something. ("The phone number is green ink in the upper right-hand corner of the page.")

Benefits to a paper planner
• It's faster to enter information than turning on an electronic planner. Just open to the page and jot down your notes.
• Most brands are less expensive than an electronic planner.
• You can keep old pages as a record of previous years.
• No electricity or batteries required.

Electronic

If you are a linear/digital person, you would probably do very well with an electronic planner. Clues that you are a linear/digital person are:
• Your thinking flows easily typing into a keyboard or through a stylus.
• You're more likely to look for something through a word search than trying to remember where you might have stored it.
• You have a good memory for dates, numbers, and chronology without needing a visual overview of a whole month or week to picture it.

Benefits to an electronic planner
• It's lightweight and compact.
• Information can be saved and moved without rewriting.
• Retrieval is speedy—just type in a key word and search.
• It can be backed up on to your computer.

Choice #2: Size

Portability is essential for teens on the go—your planner must fit in your backpack and/or your purse without weighing you down. Look for the smallest planner you can find that takes into account the number of daily to-dos you want to track, as well as the size of your handwriting. If your handwriting is large, pick a planner with bigger pages or a small one that provides a full page per day.

Choice #3: Format and Features

All planners, paper or electronic, come with a dizzying array of features and page layouts—many of which you do not need. Here are the basics you should look for.

Monthly

MUST HAVE

• ***Monthly calendar view***. *Use for class and after-school schedules, doctors' appointments, test and due dates, as well as vacation and school holidays.*

CHOOSE BETWEEN

Weekly

• ***Weekly close-up***. *For specific daily plans, calls, chores, homework assignments. Works for a maximum of five to-dos per day, without much room for notes.*
or

Daily

• ***Daily close-up***. *For specific daily plans, calls, chores, homework assignments. Works for up to twelve to-dos per day, with plenty of room for notes.*

OPTIONAL EXTRAS

• **Lists section**. For tracking to-dos by category. You can keep running lists of homework assignments by class; a list of to-dos for personal projects; lists of calls to return, letters to write, activities to do with friends; lists of items and supplies you need to buy. This is a good feature to have in both your paper and electronic planners.

• **Address section**. To use for phone numbers, addresses, e-mails, and other contact information; a good feature to have in your paper planner. You can organize it alphabetically, by first or last name—just make a decision on which and then be consistent. Both paper and electronic planners will usually come equipped with their own address section.

• **Extras**. Items such as expense envelopes and project worksheets come with paper planners; budget trackers, calculators, mapquest, timers, and/or games can be nice but not necessary with electronic planners. Select the features you know will be helpful and delete the rest to avoid being distracted from the main purpose of your planner.

Wall Calendars and Computer Calendars

Wall calendars can be as effective as a supplement to a portable datebook or electronic planner. Hung on the wall over your desk at home, they give you a quick visual overview of the month so you can keep your eye on upcoming events, due dates, and holidays. This way, you don't have to leaf through any pages to see when your big project is due and how many days you have left to work on it.

There are also free calendar programs available on the Internet. These can take the place of a wall calendar, but require your computer to be on to use it. In any case, a portable planner is still required for organizing and tracking your daily to-dos and obligations.

Setting Up and Using Your Planner

No matter which planner you choose, spend at least one to two hours customizing it when you first get it. Decide exactly where you are going to record different types of information. Where, for instance, will you schedule appointments, classes, and after-school activities? Where will you write in due dates on projects and test dates? Where will you keep your list of homework assignments? Delete the features you won't need.

Before

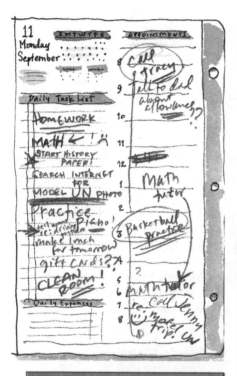

Cluttered closet

- Limited amount of space
- More stuff than storage
- Items packed into any pockets of space, in no particular order
- Haphazard arrangement makes it harder to see what you have
- Items get overlooked

Cluttered schedule

- Limited amount of hours
- More tasks than time
- Tasks jammed into pockets of time, in no particular order
- Haphazard arrangement making it harder to see what you have
- Plans and appointments get overlooked

After

TOOL #2: TIME MAP

One of the biggest challenges to organizing your schedule is learning to work with rather than against the slippery concept of time. You can't see it or hold it in your hands and it doesn't pile up like books and papers. This can make time a very difficult concept to understand.

An hour hanging out with your friends whizzes by, compared to an hour studying the periodic table of elements. As long as time remains mysterious and invisible, you will have a hard time managing your schedule. Learning to see time in more tangible, visual terms can help. Try comparing your overbooked schedule to a big cluttered closet—a limited amount of space that can fit only so much.

 Start Mapping!

Now, you'll need to determine the size of *your* week (container). In other words, how much space/time do you have to work with? Lay out your schedule on a piece of paper or on the computer. Mark the time you wake up and the time you go to sleep (be honest!). Then fill in all your classes, travel time to and from school, as well as after-school and weekend obligations such as church, sports practices, and art classes. When you have recorded all your commitments, look at the blank spaces: this is what you have to work with. Studying, social life, and family life have to be juggled in there. And while you're at it, don't forget about downtime. Everyone needs some breaks.

Consider this a work in progress. It's a good idea to keep a copy of your map with this book as you'll have a chance to revise it in subsequent chapters.

Monday	Tuesday	Wednesday	Thursday	Friday	Saturday	Sunday
Wake						
Sleep						

Define Your Priorities

Once it's all down on paper, you may be shocked to see how little time you have to work with. Or you may have more time than you thought. Just as the contents of your closet reflect your personality, the contents of your schedule reflect what's important to you. Sure, your school day takes up a lot of your time; that's built in. But you can control how you spend your free time between classes, after school, and on weekends. Make sure it reflects your priorities.

Time management from the inside out allows you to build a schedule that's a custom fit, based on what your priorities are. What are the most important activities to you? The truth is, your priorities may change from year to year as you learn more about yourself and what is available in the world. The key is to identify and accept what your priorities are right now. They become the foundation for how you spend your time.

Here are four teens with completely different priorities. It should come as no surprise that the way they spend their time reflects these vast differences. Look at how much they vary.

Emily R., 15, Virginia	Kira S., 17, Ohio
1. Academics	1. Guitar
2. Family life	2. Academics
3. After-school activities	3. Social life
4. Social life	4. Family life
5. Relaxing	5. Relaxing
6. Other—Pets	6. After-school activities
Lisa W., 18, New York	**Heather G., 14, Texas**
1. Religion	1. Family life
2. Family life	2. Academics
3. Social life	3. Relaxing
4. Academics	4. Social life
5. Relaxing	5. After-school activities

What are *your* priorities? Rate the following in order of importance from 1 to 5.

_____ Academics
_____ Social life
_____ After-school activities
_____ Relaxing
_____ Family life

Track Your Time

Now's the time to ask: How do you spend the hours between your classes and obligations? Are those open slots in your schedule planned out in advance or do you decide what to do with that time on a whim? Do the choices you make with your time reflect what is truly important to you?

To find out, track your time for one week. Make a copy of your time map and keep it with you at all times, filling in everything you do with your open time.

	Monday	Tuesday	Wednesday	Thursday	Friday	Saturday	Sunday
			Blank Time Map				
Wake							
8:00			SCHOOL				
8:30							
9:00							
9:30							
10:00							
10:30							
11:00			LUNCH				
11:30							
12:00			SCHOOL				
12:30							
1:00							
1:30							
2:00							
2:30							
3:00							
3:30							
4:00							
4:30							
5:00							
5:30							
6:00							
6:30							
7:00							
7:30							
8:00							
8:30							
9:00							
9:30							
10:00							
Sleep							

Copy or create a blank schedule grid on your computer like the one above so you can begin to plan how you spend your time. Once you have filled in the basics (see example on page 147), make several copies to work with as you read through Chapters 8, 9, and 10.

How Much Time Do You Have?

	Monday	Tuesday	Wednesday	Thursday	Friday	Saturday	Sunday
Wake 8:00						Travel	
8:30			SCHOOL				
9:00						Applause	
9:30		Free Period		Free Period			
10:00						(28 West	
10:30						27th Street,	
11:00			LUNCH			between 6th	
11:30						& Broadway)	
12:00			SCHOOL				
12:30							
1:00						Travel	Travel
1:30							
2:00							Steps
2:30	Travel	Travel	Travel				(Broadway &
3:00	Creative	Vocal (46th				Brdwy Dnce	75th)
3:30	Arts Studio	Broadway)				Cntr (57th	Travel
4:00		Travel		Travel		Broadway)	
4:30	(17 Bergen		BDC (57th			Travel	
5:00	Street,	Steps on	Broadway)	Steps on			
5:30	Brooklyn)	Broadway	Travel	Broadway		Steps	
6:00						(Broadway &	
6:30	Travel	(Broadway &	Papi	(Broadway &		75th)	
7:00		75th)	(Brooklyn)	75th)		Travel	
7:30		Travel					
8:00							
8:30							
9:00							
9:30				Travel			
10:00							

Find out how much free time you have in your schedule by plugging in your school hours, extracurricular activities, travel time, and regular appointments. The open spaces are all you have available to divide between homework, hobbies, relaxation, friends, and family. Carefully planning those hours is the key to feeling balanced and in control.

Where Does the Time Go?

	Monday	Tuesday	Wednesday	Thursday	Friday	Saturday	Sunday
6:30 Wake	Shower	Dress	Breakfast				Sleep late
8:00			SCHOOL			Chores	
8:30							
9:00							
9:30		Math		Math			Church
10:00		homework		homework			
10:30							
11:00			LUNCH				
11:30							Video
12:00			SCHOOL				games
12:30						Skateboarding	with sister
1:00							
1:30							
2:00							
2:30	Music class	Hang out	Internship	Volunteer	Snack		Shoot
3:00							hoops with
3:30		Band		Band	Nap		Dad
4:00	Homework						
4:30	Science						Reading
5:00		On-line		Homework		Shower	
5:30				Research			
6:00							
6:30			DINNER				
7:00							
7:30	Hang out	Homework	On-line	Homework	Hang out	Movies	TV
8:00	with	Social Studies		English	with	with	
8:30	sister	Science	Homework	research	friends	friends	
9:00	Homework	English	Reading	paper			On-line
9:30	Reading		Spanish				
10:00							
Sleep							

To understand where you time goes, track how you spend all of your "open" time for one week directly onto a copy of your time map. Do your choices reflect your priorities? Are you getting to everything you want to? Chapters 8, 9, and 10 will help you make clear and confident choices about how to spend your "open" time.

Evaluate Your Time Map

At the end of the week, evaluate how you've spent your time. Does your schedule reflect your priorities? If academics was #1 on your list, does it take up most of your time? Was there a lot of time you couldn't account for? What was your biggest surprise?

---

1. My biggest surprise was _____

   _____

2. I'm proud of the way I _____

   _____

3. Something I'd like to change is _____

   _____

4. My biggest time wasters are _____

   _____

5. One thing I wish I had more time for is _____

   _____

6. One thing I want to spend less time on is _____

   _____

If you are unhappy with the way you are spending your open time, don't worry. This book will help. You'll find helpful tips for balancing your time and maximizing your productivity in each major area of your life in Chapters 8, 9, and 10.

TOOL #3: THE WADE FORMULA— PUTTING IT ALL TOGETHER

The SPACE formula helps you sort through the physical piles in your life: the clothes, books, papers, and stuff. The WADE formula helps you sort through your many to-dos.

With so little time, how do you choose between the massive number of tasks you face on a given day? Here's the formula:

W.A.D.E.

Write it down in your planner.

Add it up. Estimate how long each task will take. Break large projects down into small parts for easier calculations.

Decide when you will do tasks. If overloaded, you can elect to delete, delay, diminish, or delegate them into shorter tasks.

Execute your plan. Put your plan into action without being held back by procrastination or perfectionism.

Write It Down

Tips for Calculating How Long an Activity Will Take

There are two main ways to effectively calculate the duration of each activity.

Study yourself. Assign each to-do in your planner an estimated time. As you complete each task, watch the clock, and record the actual time next to the estimate. After about two weeks, you should have a better idea of how long things actually take and how far off your estimates tend to be.

Task	Estimated Time	Actual Time
Trip to library	30 minutes	45 minutes
Dance rehearsal	1 hour	1 hour 30 minutes
Doctor visit	2 hours	1 hour 45 minutes
English paper	3 hours	1 hour 15 minutes

Overestimate time. Take the pressure off yourself by giving yourself a 50 percent cushion to finish each project (e.g., for a 1 hour task, give yourself 1 hour and 30 minutes) or even doubling the time you think it will take. This way, you can relax and concentrate to your heart's content. If you happen to finish early, all the better—you'll have some bonus free time to do with as you like.

Write It Down

You can't rely on your memory alone when it comes to keeping track of everything you need to do. It's important to record every assignment, meeting, phone call, letter, and project in your planner. For example, if you want to shop for new sneakers next Saturday, simply turn to the "Saturday, October 14" page in your planner or Palm Pilot, choose a time to go, and mark it as an appointment.

Some people prefer to keep a master to-do list in a section in the back of their planner, organized by category. For example, you can allot one page for school assignments, one for friends and family, and another for chores or job-related tasks. This allows you to capture every idea that occurs to you. You can then go back and decide how to handle all your to-dos. With electronic planners, you could use the to-do list function, categorizing each entry. In either case, when you create a master list, you will have to eventually go back to handpick the ones you will do and write them into specific day and time slots in your calendar.

Add It Up

The most common time-management problem people run into is basing their to-do list on only one question: "What do I need to do?" What's missing is the other magic question: "How long will it take?"

If time is a limited container, then each task with which you decide to fill your day has a time value. So many of us have a habit of saying, "That'll take me two seconds," whether we're talking about our math homework, our chores, or making a call. There are very few tasks that actually take two seconds. On the other hand, there are dreaded tasks you think will take forever, even though in reality they'll be done in fifteen minutes. If you can learn to accurately calculate how long something will take, then you can be realistic in planning your day.

Decide When

Once you decide to complete a to-do task, your next question becomes "When am I going to do it?" Be specific about when you will do things. Record each of your to-dos in your planner directly onto the day you intend to do them. If chores and to-dos are not tagged for a particular day or time, they are unlikely to get done. By slotting tasks into your open times on specific days, you can visualize how much your day is filling up. This will let you know when you are exceeding the space available, and setting up an impossible workload.

Of course, once you consolidate your to-dos and start to plug them into your days, you may discover that you have many more tasks than time available. When you reach the limits of your time, you need to make some trimming decisions. Here are the choices that will help you create a more doable plan.

The Four D's

• **Delete tasks**. For those of us who want to do everything and be everywhere, it's critical to make an effort to distinguish between what's truly important and what's not. Come on, do you really need to go see *Titanic* for the third time? Must you roll all your coins from your penny jar? Is it imperative that you re-cover all your books just to make them look prettier? Which tasks just don't matter that much? Once you've isolated a few potential tasks, just cross them off your list. Now, breathe a sigh of relief.

• **Delay tasks**. Even if you've determined that something is ultra-important, ask yourself, Can it wait? Can it be postponed until another day or another week? Reorganizing your video collection is probably a good idea, but do you have to do it on the one day when you have to finish your chores, prep for a midterm, and go to soccer practice? Delaying does not mean procrastinating. It means prioritizing tasks based on their due dates and urgency.

• **Diminish tasks**. Here's where it gets a bit tricky. Provided you're a responsible teen who takes your obligations seriously, there is absolutely nothing wrong with always looking for the most efficient, streamlined way to complete a task. To clarify: Diminishing your workload is not about taking shortcuts or cheating. What it *is* about is becoming a more efficient person.

Many high-achieving teens approach all their tasks with perfection in mind. But when time is limited, you need to be able to find the quickest way to your goal—rather than not doing it at all. For instance, if you're way behind on a history paper and have only a few days to prepare, you may need to reduce your research sources from five to three. If you are in a crunch studying for a test, how about focusing only on those sections brought up in a class lecture. If you are putting together a contact sheet for your volunteer group, skip everyone's street addresses and zip codes and stick to the basics: name, phone number, and e-mail address. Note: It's not wise to make a habit of diminishing tasks. This technique is to be used only when you have too much work to do and not enough time.

• **Delegate tasks**. As a teen, you probably don't have too many people with whom to share your workload. Yet learning to delegate is one of the most important and valuable time-management skills for life. Learn it now, because it's a skill you'll use often as an adult.

If something absolutely must get done and you don't have time, try to find someone who can help you. For example, if you can't attend a youth group meeting, have a friend take notes for you and return the favor if he/she is ever in the same bind.

Keep in mind that delegating, like diminishing tasks, is not something you do to avoid your responsibilities; it's a technique you use to fulfill them. In other words, if it's your job to take out the garbage every day, and you have a late band practice, asking your sibling to cover for you is the responsible thing to do. In selecting who will do the task you're delegating, consider if they have the skills, knowledge, and sense of responsibility to do it well, and then follow up to make sure it got done. Give them brief instructions on what is most important in carrying out the task. If you find someone who is more knowledgeable than you in getting a task done, take the opportunity to learn from them, so that the next time, you can improve upon your own performance.

Execute Your Plan

There's an old saying: "Plan your work, then work your plan." There's no point in putting all this thought into what you are going to do if you aren't going to implement your plan. This means completing the tasks you set forth on the days you decided to do them. It also means starting and finishing projects according to plan. As we zero in on studying, after-school activities, and social life in the following chapters, we'll give you guidelines on avoiding procrastination, lateness, and interruptions that can ruin the best-laid plans.

So, are there any questions? You probably have a million. Don't worry, Chapters 8, 9, and 10 will make it clear.

8

Studying

Project Checklist for Organizing Your Study Schedule	
MATERIALS	Planner
	Time map
	List of priorities
ESTIMATED TIME	1–2 hours

Deadlines, exams, essays, and pop quizzes are facts of everyday life for most teens. That's why it's so important to figure out how to maximize your study time so you can get your work done on deadline, at the quality level you want, and still leave time for the other activities in your life. In this chapter, we will ask you to consider a variety of factors to customize your system, such as your best times for studying, ideal working conditions, and the amount of time various assignments consume. You'll be surprised at how much you can get done when you take stock of your particular habits and needs, and find a study schedule that works for you.

PHASE 1: ANALYZE

It's time to step back and assess your current homework situation. By asking the same four questions introduced in Chapter 2, you'll be well on your way to understanding how to get the most out of your study time.

Question #1: What's Working and What's Not?

Get specific about which areas of your homework are causing problems and which aren't. This will help you learn about your strengths as a student and limit your efforts to the areas that need fixing.

For each subject, indicate which types of homework are

+ **Working.** You get it done efficiently and are happy with the process and the results *or*
− **Not working.** You don't get it done on time, don't like the process, and/or are unhappy with the results.

Use the following inventory to guide you.

Math	_____ Daily homework _____ Long-term projects _____ Reading _____ Studying for tests _____ Other:
English	_____ Daily homework _____ Long-term projects _____ Reading _____ Studying for tests _____ Other:
Social studies	_____ Daily homework _____ Long-term projects _____ Reading _____ Studying for tests _____ Other:
Science	_____ Daily homework _____ Long-term projects _____ Reading _____ Studying for tests _____ Other:
Foreign language	_____ Daily homework _____ Long-term projects _____ Reading _____ Studying for tests _____ Other:

💬 "I put big assignments, like research papers, off until the last minute, and then have to rush them in the end."

—Alicia F., 16, Michigan

Reviewing your answers, ask yourself if there is a pattern to your homework struggles. Are you usually good with daily homework but not on long-term projects? Is reading a problem because you always fall asleep? Do you do better at projects that excite you than the boring daily stuff? Are some teachers more inspiring than others . . . and does this affect your performance? What can you learn from your strengths that will help you improve on your weak areas?

Question #2: What's Your Essential 7?

When it comes to getting homework done, determining the Essential 7 involves identifying your best times and conditions for studying. Think about it: What conditions make getting your homework done quickly and stress free? Is it your CD player? Good lighting? Tuning into your energy cycles can also help you make the most of your study time. Identifying your Essential 7 will help you get your work done quickly, swiftly, and at the level of quality you want.

To help you get started, we've included a list of Essential 7s for two very different teens.

Studying Essentials	
James B., 17, Kentucky	Kaci M., 15, Illinois
1. Desk	1. Bed
2. Privacy	2. Study buddy
3. Good lighting	3. Dim lighting
4. Flash cards	4. Textbooks
5. Snacks	5. Gum
6. Quiet	6. Music
7. Tension ball	7. Review sheets

Energy Drainers versus Energy Boosters

Obviously, your peak energy times and your free time aren't always going to coincide, and you may have more homework hours than natural peak energy times. Good time managers know how to boost, pace, and protect their energy throughout the day.

It's important to identify what drains your energy and what fuels it. In other words, when your concentration starts to flag, you must determine what gets you right back to work, as opposed to what distracts you and uses up all your energy.

Energy drainers	Energy boosters
Skipping meals	Eating three healthy meals
Soda	Water
Watching TV	Exercise
Junk Food	Vitamins
Not enough sleep	Short nap
Add your own here:	*Add your own here:*

CHART YOUR ENERGY CYCLES

Natural energy

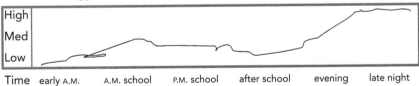

Based on your own energy cycles, determine the best times for tackling your toughest studying tasks. For example, if you concentrate best during the day, consider using free periods during school hours to do your homework. That would clear your nights to spend any way you wish without feeling obligated to do homework. If you're a night owl, you can set aside time to study after dinner and use your free daylight hours for other activities without feeling guilty.

Jessi Says

My Studying Essential 7

1. *Peace and quiet!* I have tried for years to get away with listening to music while studying, swearing (to no one but myself) that it helps me block out other distractions and puts me at a place of ease. I am kidding no one—when I pop Tom Petty into my CD player, I don't care how big the test is, I have to get up and belt out "And I'm FREEEEEEEEEEEE, Free Fallin'!" to my entire neighborhood at that very moment.

2. *Pen and a lot of paper.* One of the best ways for me to memorize things is to have it just plain drilled into my head. One of my favorite ways of doing this is to write it over and over again. Continually putting it down chisels the info into my head, and if I feel shaky on it, I write it at the top of my class notes the next day before beginning class or at the top of the test I am studying for as soon as I receive it.

3. *Flash cards.* This is my other favorite way of drilling something into my head. I copy down all the appropriate info onto flash cards (questions on the front and answers on the back), shuffle them up, and go through the pile, just reading over the information. Then I go through it and try to guess each answer. After that, I go through the pile a third time and separate the cards I've memorized from the ones I got wrong. I keep going through the pile that I haven't yet memorized until it disappears. Finally, I go through all the cards one more time to be positive that I have them all memorized.

4. *Good class notes.* These are the basis for my studying. If I don't get good notes in class, I borrow some from a friend. Without them, creating any study mechanism is impossible and has no point of reference.

5. *Immersion.* If I'm studying a lot of new information all at once, I need to be surrounded by it completely. To do this, I turn my apartment into one humongous quiz. I post flash cards everywhere, with just the question facing outward. Anytime I want to do something, I have to first answer the question. For example, if "What does *gato* mean?" is on the refrigerator, I can't open it until I answer correctly: "cat."

6. *Study buddy!* The night before a test, I usually get on the phone with a friend who's in the same class and we take turns explaining the concepts and processes to each other. This helps both the explainer and the explainee to understand and make meaning of the content.

7. *Glass of water.* A glass of water is essential to me on multiple levels when studying. For one, it distracts me from any hunger due to boredom that may occur while studying. Having cool water also prevents me from feeling fried or losing focus because of overconcentration. Last, once I have finished a glass of water, I have to go refill it, giving me a minute of breathing room from the material I'm studying.

Question #3: What's the Payoff?

Studying takes major discipline. When the work piles on, it's easy to wonder what the purpose of studying is. Is it the pleasure of learning, or just to get a good grade and then forget the content? There are some subjects that you love, and others that you think are boring and useless. Add to that the growing burden of having to take all those standardized tests (PSATs and SATs). It's not unusual to get overwhelmed. The key is to keep yourself motivated during every study session.

Defining your big-picture goals can keep you on track during high- and low-energy cycles, especially when the pressure is on. Now's your chance to think about what makes you want to do well in school and what you're hoping to get out of it. Here are some ideas to get your started.

- "To eliminate the stress of last-minute cramming sessions."
  —Stacy K., 14, Arizona

- "I want to shorten my studying (and procrastination) time so that I have more time for other activities."
  —Mikhall W., 15, Wyoming

- "To gain freedom and trust from my parents."
  —Penny L., 17, Pennsylvania

- "To get a scholarship for college."
  —Lloyd D., 14, New Jersey

💬 "To figure out what career I want to pursue."

—Kelly N., 18, Colorado

💬 "When I get sick of the homework routine, I discipline myself by thinking about the deal I made to attend soccer camp if I maintain a B average. It gets me going every time."

—Jeremy T., 14, Michigan

Question #4: What's the Problem?

If you're always turning your homework in late, losing assignments, and missing out on study time, you probably think it's because you're just not a good student. But by zeroing in on the specific obstacles getting in your way, you will instantly find yourself on the road to a solution.

In Chapter 1 we introduced a set of roadblocks that often prevent teens from getting organized. When it comes to studying, those apply as well as some new ones.

Read through the following obstacles and check the boxes next to the ones that sound like your issues.

❑ Forgetting assignments	❑ More tasks than time	❑ Procrastination
❑ Miscalculating time required	❑ Disorganized study space	❑ Perfectionism
❑ Frequent interruptions	❑ Overwhelming assignments	❑ Unclear goals and priorities

PHASE 2: STRATEGIZE

Now that you have analyzed your current state of studying, you can start planning strategies to improve your ability to manage your study time.

✎ Julie's Work Journal:

Daniel's Story

Daniel was a very smart, dynamic student who really wanted to do well in school. But no matter how many times he tried to complete work ahead of time, he always found himself waiting until the eleventh hour to tackle his homework assignments. He was often able to do high-quality work at the last minute—he'd sometimes start a history project or paper the night before it was due, get really into it, and pull off a great paper. But working all night meant other projects and homework were neglected, and he'd get F's on those. Adding to the problem, staying up all night often caused him to over-sleep the next day—and he'd end up getting his paper in a day late anyway and losing a grade point for lateness. In short, Daniel's last-minute approach was working against him, affecting both his grades and his energy level.

As I spoke with Daniel, we realized that he thrives on that pressure. When he gave himself time to work on a project at a leisurely pace, he couldn't get started, was overly obsessed about the details, and couldn't make progress until he was almost out of time. Time pressure energized Daniel, and in a strange way it relaxed him, keeping him from being paralyzed by his tendency to be a perfectionist. By waiting until the last minute, he figured he had a built-in explanation if the end result wasn't extraordinary.

Instead of fighting this need for pressure, we decided to work with it. We decided that Daniel would make it his personal mission to complete every assignment *on the day it was assigned.* This would apply to daily homework as well as longer-term projects. For instance, if his English teacher assigned an essay on a Tuesday with a due date of the following Monday, Dan would knock himself silly to get it done by Tuesday night.

If the project was impossible to finish in one night, he would break the assignment down into three to five steps, and commit to doing the first step that night. This way, at least he had the project started, and he would complete the subsequent steps over the course of the next few days, always aiming to get the project done as close to the *assignment* date (rather than the *due* date) as possible.

This provided as much "last-minute pressure" as Daniel needed to get things done, but in the process allowed him to get the work finished in advance. This way, he was sure not to miss any assignments, and in the event any unexpected crisis came up, he was not derailed. By working in advance, he always had extra time the day or two before the assignment's due date to put his perfectionism to work—bringing his grades up from a B to an A. Daniel made the adjustment quickly, and his grades benefited without his having to change his natural work style.

Adjust Your Time Map

Look at the time map you created in Chapter 7. Examine the time slots currently devoted to homework. Are there enough? Are they at your peak energy time? Based on what you learned about yourself in the "Analyze" section, what changes can you make to your study schedule to improve your chances for success?

Questions to Ask Yourself

- Am I setting aside enough time for studying and homework?
- Could I adjust my study schedule to make better use of my energy cycles?
- Are there unused free times in my schedule that can be earmarked specifically for studying?
- Are there any nonschool activities I can cut to open up more room for homework?
- Can I subdivide large open times into sections, designating part of the time for studying and leaving the rest for another kind of activity?

PHASE 3: ATTACK

OK, it's a fact that you will be given new assignments every day. But why is it that all five of your teachers seem to decide to give you a three-hour workload on the same night? They usually don't seem to communicate with one another. School is just set up that way. You'll have one night with practically no homework, and then the next day it might be completely overwhelming.

To keep your system under control and prepare for all kinds of studying emergencies, you'll need to apply the WADE formula to sort through the workload. Now, let's get to it!

STEP 1: WRITE IT DOWN

Designate a space in your planner for recording assignments. Some students write assignments down on the day they are assigned. Others write them on the day they are due (but that can be dangerous–you may forget to work on the assignments on the days leading up to the due date). Some mark both places. Still others record all their assignments in their to-do section in their Palm Pilot or planner, until they figure out when they are going to fulfill the job.

Wherever you choose to record them, be consistent so that you always know where to find the information you need. Also, be sure to fill in all the details, so you are not stuck at the last minute without instructions or relevant details about how to complete the assignment.

> 💬 "Make a list of every single little thing that you have to do that day. Then check it off as you do it."
> –Erica J., 13, Missouri

> 💬 "Take notes on things that the teachers put a special emphasis on."   –Ashley H., 14, Virginia

STEP 2: ADD IT UP

Once your assignments are written down, you'll need to estimate how long each will take to complete. This isn't always as easy as it might seem. There are quick projects and long projects. There are speedy approaches and more thorough techniques–including the overly obsessive approach, in which you spend ten hours belaboring a two-hour task.

For each assignment, it's important to ask yourself: (1) How long should this take? and (2) How long do I want to give it? The most important thing to remember is: Be realistic! Don't give in to wishful thinking. Accept that some assignments will be quick and others will require setting aside a significant block of time. Bottom line: That ten-page history paper is not going to get researched, outlined, and written in two hours–and you know it.

At the beginning of each semester try to assess your workload. It's important to look for cues from your teachers; each one has a different pattern of assigning homework and administering tests. You also need to take into consideration the fact that some new subjects may throw you for a loop. Algebra goes fast for some teens, slow for others. You'll need to factor in your own unique pace before estimating how much time you'll be devoting to each subject.

Special Circumstances:
LONG-TERM PROJECTS

Starting in junior high school, assignments begin to get more complicated and involved. There are three-hundred-page novels to get through, research projects to carry out over a two-month period, and multipage essay papers to write.

> "When trying to get all of my reading done for class, I find it easiest to sit down and take some time to actually analyze what I have to read. That way, I know how long all of the assignments are in advance, so I can space out my time in reading them instead of reading three hundred pages the night before an assignment is due."   —Amanda R., 18, Pennsylvania

Calculating how much time a long-term project will take isn't easy—in fact, it's one of the biggest time-management challenges that exists. But mastering this skill will make you a highly valued employee, business owner, or head of household someday.

The trick is not to do everything in one sitting, but to break large projects into simple, manageable baby steps.

All calculations need to include a "margin of error." This means that you should always aim to complete your assignments at least a few days before they are due, so you can give yourself time to review, edit, and analyze your work. The margin of error is also important because you never know when a teacher will unexpectedly dump another huge workload in your lap due immediately! By finishing up your long-term projects early, you'll be able to handle these sorts of surprises.

Let's say you have a research paper due in three weeks. How might you break that down into manageable steps? Calculate the time, then mark your study sessions in your calendar/planner.

Research Paper Time Estimate

Assignment: Wedding rituals in Japanese modern culture (due in 3 weeks)

Research	4 hours
Write	3 hours
Revise	2 hours
Total time: 9 hours	Hand in: Friday

Research Paper Schedule

	Sunday	Monday	Tuesday	Wednesday	Thursday	Friday	Saturday
Week 1		research 2 hours			research 2 hours		
Week 2			write 1 hour		write 1 hour	write 1 hour	
Week 3		revise 1 hour		revise 1 hour		**DUE DATE**	

OK, you're next up for a huge reading assignment. How can you approach that? Calculate the number of pages per night and log it in your planner.

Reading Time Estimate

Assignment:	Read **Great Expectations** (500 pages)
Due date	April 6
Number of days till due date	14 days
Cushion	4 days
Total days to complete assignment	10
Total # pages:	500 pages / 10 days = 50 pages per night

Reading Schedule

Assignment: Read **Great Expectations** (500 pages) in 14 days

3/24	3/25	3/26	3/27	3/28	3/29	3/30
50 pages	50 pages	50 pages	50 pages	50 pages	50 pages	50 pages
3/31	4/1	4/2	4/3	4/4	4/5	4/6
50 pages	50 pages	50 pages	Review	Review	Review	Due

Finally, you have a huge midterm. Here's an example of how to plan your studying so you're confident on the big day.

Test Study Prep

Assignment: Science midterm (200 pages of material)

Test date	November 20
Weeks till test	12
Less 2-week cushion	= 10 weeks
Total # pages	200 pages / 10 weeks
	= 20 pages per week
Pace	10 pages per hour (read, outline, review)
Total study time	26 hours divided into 2 or 3 weekly installments

Test Study Schedule

Assignment: Science midterm (200 pages of material) 12 weeks to study

Wk 1	2	3	4	5	6	7	8	9	10	11	12
20 pages	20 pages	20 pages	20 pages	20 pages	20 pages	20 pages	20 pages	20 pages	20 pages	review	review
2 hours	2 hours	2 hours	2 hours	2 hours	2 hours	2 hours	2 hours	2 hours	2 hours	3 hours	3 hours

Pace: 10 pages in 1 hour (read, outline, review)
Total study time: 26 hours, 3 hours per week

After reviewing our examples, take a stab at breaking down your assignments.

When it comes to estimating reading time, don't rely solely on the number of pages. Some longer novels read like the wind, while that slim Shakespeare tragedy can take forever. When tackling any new book, conduct a trial run by timing yourself as you read the first ten pages. That will give an indication of the pace for reading the rest of the book.

The following example illustrates how each student works at his/her own pace. Jasmin and Adam are in the same classes and get the same homework yet require a different amount of time for each subject. It's important to determine your own unique pace and work with it.

Daily Homework

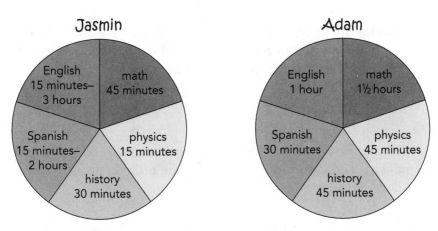

Jasmin

English 15 minutes– 3 hours
math 45 minutes
Spanish 15 minutes– 2 hours
physics 15 minutes
history 30 minutes

Adam

English 1 hour
math 1½ hours
Spanish 30 minutes
physics 45 minutes
history 45 minutes

STEP 3: DECIDE WHEN

There's no way around it: Every new day brings new assignments. Some need to be completed by the next day. Others are more long-term. Making smart, proactive decisions about what to do will keep you feeling on top of your homework. Use the following considerations to figure out how to prioritize your time.

• **Urgency.** Make the activity with the earliest and most pressing due date your top priority. If you have a research paper due in one week, make sure you get started immediately.

• **Variety.** Vary your activities to keep your energy high and yourself engaged. For example, if you've been reading for three hours, it may help to change activities to something more interactive.

• **Significance.** Each time you sit down to study, ask yourself which one assignment will give you the greatest sense of satisfaction to get done. Tackling the most challenging and important assignments first will give you the greatest sense of relief and accomplishment.

• **Duration.** If you have only thirty minutes, select an assignment that can be completed in that time frame. For example, use the time for a list of math problems or chemistry equations, or to complete a short reading assignment. If you've got a two-hour block of time, use it for a long assignment, such as writing an essay.

• **Energy level.** As described in this chapter, we all have natural energy cycles and moments when we can concentrate better than others. Select a task that matches your energy level to make the most out of the time available.

The Four D's

OK! Let's say all your teachers pile the homework on in a single night. The load is suddenly too big for the time allotted. What can you do? Choose one or more of the following:

• **Delete tasks.** And by this we don't mean homework assignments. During especially busy periods of the school year, you can cut back on social engagements and activities like organizing your stamp collection to free up more time for your schoolwork.

• **Delay tasks.** Postpone appointments and activities that are not urgent. If you know you have a Spanish exam the next morning and your English paper is not due for a week, delay working on your paper until you've had time to study for your test. Just make sure to jump right on the paper as soon as the test is over, so you don't end up cramming your English assignment too close to deadline.

- **Diminish tasks.** When you have absolutely no time and need to finish something quickly, create shortcuts, like listening to books on tape if you're a slow reader, or speeding through a first draft of your essay and asking a friend to proofread it for you.

- **Delegate tasks.** If you have a study group, split up the work. (Make sure the group works well together; otherwise you may wind up doing more than your fair share of the work.) Or, if you're especially pressed for time, ask your parents and/or siblings to pitch in with your share of the chores. Make sure to return the favor when your mom, dad, or sibling is in a hurry.

STEP 4: EXECUTE YOUR PLAN

Now that you've planned your study schedule, it's time to make it happen. What could possibly stop you now? Unfortunately *a lot!* This is the Danger Zone—a lot of people fail at this stage because of the constant challenges we are bombarded with along the way to executing our plans. There are three common culprits that get in your way. Think of these obstacles as the asteroids in a video game. Just as you must avoid the asteroids to reach the treasure, there are hurdles that must be cleared in order to successfully complete your homework.

By identifying these in advance, you can anticipate and recognize them when they appear, and quickly extinguish them before they block the finish line.

Culprit #1: Interruptions
Interruptions come in all shapes and sizes. You know how it goes. Just as you sit down to study for that chemistry final, your kid brother bursts into your room and demands a PlayStation rematch. Or you've gathered all your research materials and are about to

Tips for Minimizing Interruptions

• Ask if it can wait. Most interruptions can be put off until your preplanned break. (It can be helpful to plan a short break every hour or two so nothing important has to wait too long.)

• Pick the right time to study. Don't sit down for a long study session right before dinner or in the middle of your sibling's drum lesson.

• Gather snacks and supplies in advance to avoid interrupting yourself once you've started.

• Work in a library.

• Keep your planner handy, to instantly record every distracting reminder, idea, and to-do that pops into your head. By writing thoughts down where you can find them later, you won't be tempted to stop in the middle of your study session to complete them.

• Surf the Internet incognito. Avoid instant messages while doing Internet research by signing on under a different e-mail name. Or shut off your IM while on-line.

• Let your answering machine or voice mail take your calls and return them when you have time.

• Don't panic. When something unexpected happens, stay flexible and don't stress out. (Things will come up!) If you're in control in general, you don't need to worry about a few setbacks.

dive into that global studies project, when "Ring!" It's your friend calling with urgent news. Or your mom needs your help setting the table.

All interruptions are not external—sometimes we interrupt ourselves because we get bored with our task and lose concentration after a certain period of time. Let's say you're reading along in your sociology textbook when an idea pops into your head about a research paper in history. You might be tempted to stop your sociology reading in that moment and instantly start surfing the Net for that research paper. Or you're busy doing math when all of a sudden you remember that you need to return your best friend's call about that ten dollars you owe her. If you stop to handle every interruption the minute it comes up, you will never get your homework done, and you will lose a lot of time trying to remember where you were when you got sidetracked.

Culprit #2: Procrastination and Lateness

Procrastination and lateness are without a doubt the biggest enemies of a successfully planned day. When you get a late start, one task spills over into the next, leaving many of the items on your to-do list undone.

To make matters worse, we usually procrastinate by doing insignificant tasks that are truly a waste of our time. In the end, you wind up spending a lot of time doing nothing but feeling angry at yourself for not accomplishing what you set out to do. This self-defeating cycle drains your positive energy and makes it even harder to move on to the next important thing on your list.

Here are some techniques that can help you overcome the destructive forces of procrastination and lateness.

• Start small. If you lack confidence about doing a project well, just focus on the first step. Will Smith says he's built his entire successful career on the lessons his father taught him about building a wall, one brick at a time.

• For truly dreaded tasks, approach them in thirty-minute increments. At the end of that time period, give yourself the option to either move on to something else or keep going if (surprise!) you are really into it.

• Do the biggest task first. Starting your homework session with lots of small, easy tasks drains and diffuses your energy. The relief you get from accomplishing the hardest task first will help you speed through the rest of your homework.

• Take the pressure off. Instead of trying to do things *perfectly* the first time, just *do* them. If you have time left over, you can always go back and refine.

• Combine unappealing assignments with things you actually enjoy doing (like listening to new CDs while doing chemistry homework or working with a group).

• Focus on the payoff. If you hate an assignment, remind yourself why you want to do well—to get to soccer camp or go out on Saturday night.

• Ask for help. There's bound to be a study buddy, tutor, or teacher who can help you with a tough assignment.

• Change your clocks. If you are always running late, set your alarm clock and watch a few minutes early. Using an odd amount of time (such as seven, twelve, or seventeen minutes) seems to prove most effective in outsmarting yourself. It takes too long to recalculate the proper time.

Culprit #3: Perfectionism

> "I have a hard time getting to all of my assignments. I am such a perfectionist that by the time I finish my English homework, there's no time to tackle history."
> —Elaine T., 15, New York

The need for perfection makes it hard to let go of a task, even once it's complete. Putting the finishing touches on an essay, for instance, you might think of a better way to word it, and another better way, and yet another. Soon you find yourself running way behind schedule or overthinking an already well-thought-out essay.

Here are some ways to control the worrywart inside of you.

• Set time limits. Deadlines force you to make decisions and inspire you not only to work but to work efficiently.

Jessi Says

Getting Through an Excruciating Essay

In tenth grade, we read *The Odyssey* by Homer. The follow-up assignment was a huge, painful thesis essay based on our reading of the book. This also involved spending a lot of time researching and reading critical essays about the book. Well, to be honest, I couldn't care less about Odysseus's dual personality or who was going to the underworld and why. We were due to hand in a first draft a week after it was assigned. Six days came and went, and suddenly it was the night before D day. I had a moderately substantial amount of research, but not a dot of ink on the page. At around 9:00 P.M., sitting in front of the computer, I found myself once again magically swept away into the world of computer solitaire. Try as I might, I simply could not get the paper started. I wrote out a few bulleted ideas on different approaches I could take, then decided instead to approach the teacher for help the next day.

My teacher looked over the itsy-bitsy bit of work that I had and offered some alternative approaches. The final draft was due in three days.

That night I went home and tried again. Nothing. The next night, the same story: still nothing. On the final night before the stupid, wretched, horrible paper was due, I began to panic. I decided that I could not write the paper well at this point, and instead I would just spit out one mediocre draft and bring it to the teacher the next day and tell her that I was in crisis. I hammered out the essay without paying any attention whatsoever to the quality. I just wanted to have something on paper. When I couldn't think of a better description than "This character sucks," I put exactly that.

When I read it over, I found that the syntax was horrible and the format was awful, but the content wasn't half bad. Once I had something to work with, I could sculpt it, weeding out the humongous kinks and filling in the mile-long gaps. The paper began to come to life.

The next day I asked for a one-day extension, and it was granted. I kneaded the paper all night and handed in an excellent version.

• Don't revise as you work. Complete one full draft and then review it once it's complete.

• Look at your entire plan before you begin. Too often perfectionists get so absorbed in the first task, they forget what else they have to do that day.

• Don't second-guess yourself. Count to ten before making difficult decisions and go with your gut instincts.

• Be a selective perfectionist. Go easy on the less significant assignments to leave more time for perfecting the ones that really matter to you—or to your transcript.

• Silence the inner critic. Don't compare your work to that of your peers. Just do your best!

Reward Yourself

Motivating yourself with little rewards is another way to ensure that you make it to the finish line. Whether you allow yourself a half hour of television for every two hours studied or treat yourself with extra time on the computer, having something waiting for you at the end of a study session will provide that extra incentive.

Instead of rushing from one project to the next, allow some time to congratulate yourself properly for every milestone reached. Tell yourself, "Once I finish this math problem, I'll take ten minutes to IM with my friends." Or, "Once I'm done researching the paper at the library, I'll reward myself with a trip to the mall." This will ensure that you keep yourself motivated even during times of stress and work overload.

And don't cancel your reward just because you've finally gotten on a roll. Keeping your promise to yourself can provide you the necessary energy and drive to keep achieving.

9

After-School Activities

Project Checklist	
MATERIALS	Planner
	Time map
	Priorities
ESTIMATED TIME	1–2 hours

For many teens, extracurricular activities can seem to play an even more significant role than school itself. Whether it's drama, debate club, sports, or playing an instrument, activities are important because they allow you to explore new ideas and pursue interests that may blossom into full-fledged careers or rewarding lifelong hobbies. Some kids also have to work after school, as well as make time for family chores and responsibilities.

It's not easy fitting in extracurricular activities. The trick is to find a way to balance them while still attending to school, friends, and family who are also all vying for attention. This chapter will discuss how to find the time for your extracurricular activities in a way that they enhance your life, rather than exhaust you.

% Fifty-eight percent of teen girls who say their lives are stressed say the stress is due to being overscheduled (in a survey sponsored by *Teen* magazine and Sears).

Teens and After-School Activities

Ever wondered what your peers are doing after school and on weekends? We've surveyed teens all over the country and here are some typical extracurricular breakdowns.

Rebecca D., 15, New York	Christina S., 13, New Jersey
School library squad and literary magazine	Band, jazz band, yearbook staff, field hockey, track, guitar, piano, trumpet
Katie K., 15, Michigan	**Cecily N., 13, Indiana**
Basketball, swimming, track and field, student council, youth advisory committee	Poetry circle, honors assembly, viola, spelling bee, youth ministry
Jed B., 16, New York	**Stacy G., 17, Missouri**
Soccer, football, orchestra, tap dancing	Basketball, school musical, choir, band, church

PHASE 1: ANALYZE

If you're having a hard time managing your after-school life, begin to take control by answering the big four questions.

Question #1: What's Working and What's Not?

When you are caught up in a whirlwind of busy-ness, it's hard to figure out what to do to fix your after-school situation. The more specific you can get about what is and isn't working about each activity, the easier it will be to address the problems.

In the first column, list your extracurricular activities. Then evaluate each one according to the criteria indicated below.

• **Enjoyment.** Are you enjoying the activity? Do you leave feeling satisfied? Sometimes we start things with high hopes, but they turn out to be a disappointment. Sometimes things we dread turn out to be great fun.

• **Goal fulfillment.** Do you have a particular goal in mind for this activity or are you just doing it because someone suggested it? If you do have a goal in mind, is the activity actually fulfilling that end? Again, some things work out better than planned; others carry surprises. (Note: If you need help defining your goals, jump down to "Question #3: What's the Payoff?")

• **Outside preparation.** Are you able to fulfill the extra preparation and responsibilities outside the meetings (e.g., background reading for debate club, fund-raising calls for boys' club, math drills for SAT prep course). Is the homework more than you expected? Has it gotten out of hand? Is it truly manageable?

For each activity, indicate which criteria are

+ **Working.** You are enjoying the activity and are happy with the process and the results *or*
– **Not working.** You aren't enjoying the activity, don't like the process, and/or are unhappy with the results.

Use the following examples to guide you.

Activity #1 *Soccer*
My goal: Stay in shape   _____ Enjoyment _____ Goal fulfillment _____ Outside preparation _____ Other:

Activity #2 *Debate Team*		
My goal: Prep for college	_____	Enjoyment
	_____	Goal fulfillment
	_____	Outside preparation
	_____	Other:

Activity #3 *After-School Job*		
My goal: Money for clothes	_____	Enjoyment
	_____	Goal fulfillment
	_____	Outside preparation
	_____	Other:

Once you have completed this survey, try to pinpoint any recurring patterns. Are you enjoying all your after-school activities equally? Are you always prepared for every activity? Is there something you are enjoying more than you'd realized? Are after-school activities interfering with your daily homework load? Asking these questions can help you home in on the activities you enjoy most and those that may be draining your energy reserves.

Question #2: What's Your Essential 7?

When it came to organizing spaces, your Essential 7 list included items you absolutely could not live without. For studying, your Essential 7 list consisted of the conditions and best times for studying. In terms of your after-school activities, your Essential 7 list should include optimal conditions for doing the activity, as well as any items you may need in the process. To help you get started, we've compiled an Essential 7 list for two teens.

After-School Essentials	
Carrie S., 16, California Swim team, dance classes	**John G., 14, Connecticut** Football team, debate club
1. Swim gear 2. Dance attire 3. Planner 4. Stretching 5. Energy bars 6. Winning attitude 7. Waterproof watch	1. Warm-up time 2. Helmet and uniform 3. Debate assignments 4. Debate partner 5. Good grades 6. Knee and elbow pads 7. Car pool

Question #3: What's the Payoff?

In considering whether to stick with an after-school activity, it's essential to define how it does (or doesn't) relate to your goals. In other words, what is your purpose in doing it? Why are you choosing to spend your free time with the kids in the art club or drama department or debate team instead of just hanging out playing video games? You should have a driving reason. It could be that you're enjoying it, getting a physical or creative outlet, helping family, developing talents, expanding your social circle, building your college résumé, investing in a career path, making a difference in the world, or developing leadership skills.

With your answers in hand, you'll be able to prioritize your activities in terms of their importance, as well as see duplication of efforts.

> "To fulfill my passion for writing and playing guitar."
> —Sandy M., 14, Kentucky

> "To stay competitive on my volleyball team so I can make the varsity squad."
> —Rachel K., 16, Illinois

> "Both Key Club and College Now are preparing me to do well once I get to college."
> —Marina V., 17, New York

💬 "As a psychology and sociology major in my freshman year of college, I look back at high school and realize that the activities I did outside of school influenced my choice of majors. My youth group meant the world to me because not only did I get to socialize with other teenagers like me, I also learned how to be a leader. I served on a committee for planning activities involving social action and community service. It is so important to find things that move you and make an impact on you because the results are life- and mind-altering." —Amanda R., 18, Maryland

Fourteen-year-old Zane S. loved fly-fishing, and decided he wanted a very expensive fly-fishing rod. The rod was $360, so he needed to figure out a way to earn enough money to buy it. He had nine weeks to save up the money before summer. His monthly allowance was $25, which would give him $50 by July. To make up the difference, he offered to do extra chores for his parents, at a rate of $6/hour if he worked five hours in a span of a week, $5/hour if he worked fewer than five hours in a week. Very motivated to get that special fishing rod, Zane set aside time on the weekends and some evenings to help his parents with cleaning out the basement, computer work, and gardening. He made his goal and felt like a million.

Once you have your answers, you'll be able to prioritize your activities in terms of their importance, as well as see duplication of goals.

Question #4: What's the Problem?

The following are the most common roadblocks that may be interfering with proper time management of your after-school activities. Take a look and check the boxes next to the obstacles that may be getting in your way.

❑ Conflicting commitments	❑ Forgetting to-dos	❑ Lack of confidence
❑ Miscalculating time required	❑ Disorganized space	❑ More tasks than time
❑ Transportation challenges	❑ Unclear goals and priorities	❑ Unsatisfying activity

✎ Julie's Work Journal:

Cecile's Story

Cecile was a bright-eyed, energetic, responsible teen who was really worried about how she was going to fit in all of the extracurriculars she wanted to do. In ninth grade, she'd already had a hard time juggling her days between drama classes, kickboxing, dance, and helping out with her little sister's Brownie troop. Moving into tenth grade, she wanted to add guitar lessons and volleyball to the mix, all this while maintaining her straight-A average, doing her chores (washing her school clothes, packing lunches, brushing the dogs), and spending time with her family, with whom she was very close. She shared a room with her younger sister, Margo, who often wanted Cecile's attention while she was doing her homework. And she had dinner with her family every night. But since her stepdad was a restaurateur, they went out to eat every night to check out the competition.

Cecile had a clear-cut case of more tasks than time. In order to accommodate additional extracurricular activities, it seemed that *something* would have to go. But there was less to delete than you'd expect. In examining all her activities, we realized that the dinners out with her family were taking two and a half hours—a huge amount of time. Instead of going out with her parents five nights a week, the family decided she and her sister could stay home and eat a simple half-hour dinner together Monday through Thursday—and they'd go out as a family on Friday nights. This freed up two hours a night for homework. Cecile also asked Margo to help her with her chores so they could hang out and get the chores done more quickly. With all the extra time together, Margo was more comfortable leaving Cecile alone to finish her homework in peace. Cecile was amazed: Not only did she get more done but she was even able to go to sleep earlier. By cutting just one task and rearranging the rest, she was able to fit in far more than she'd expected.

PHASE 2: STRATEGIZE

Great! You've completed the first step. You probably have a better handle on what's working, what's not, and how your activities fit into your big-picture goals. Now it's time to see how to make the most of your schedule to accommodate all of your activities.

◬ Adjust Your Time Map

How many activities can you handle? How many will your schedule support? Do you want to pursue many different activities or focus exclusively on the one you're most passionate about?

Take a look at the time map you created in Chapter 7. Now that you have revisited how much space you have allotted for after-school activities, you can assess ways to increase your time for these activities. Thinking back to what you discovered in the "Analyze" section, you might want to consider making some adjustment changes to your schedule.

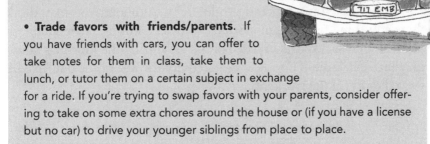

Special Circumstances:
GETTING AROUND

The issue of transportation often becomes a major sticking point for suburban kids who don't always have access to buses, subways, and the like. Here are some ways to mastermind the transportation problem in the event you don't have your driver's license, a car, or parents who are available to chauffeur you to and from your activities.

• **Carpool**. Talk to others in your activity to arrange group transportation. If you get four people involved, your mom, dad, or older sib will only have to play chauffeur on a rotating basis.

• **Trade favors with friends/parents**. If you have friends with cars, you can offer to take notes for them in class, take them to lunch, or tutor them on a certain subject in exchange for a ride. If you're trying to swap favors with your parents, consider offering to take on some extra chores around the house or (if you have a license but no car) to drive your younger siblings from place to place.

 *Finding Extra Time*

Before you give up any of your activities, see if you can find a way, by adjusting your time map, to fit everything in and still maintain a balance with your other obligations. As with an overstuffed closet, if you arrange things very carefully, you may have more room than you think.

With a little extra thinking, you can add extra hours to your extracurricular schedule. Here are a few examples of how you can accomplish this.

• Move a flexible activity to a different time slot. Can you move your private flute lessons to Thursday? Tutoring to Saturdays instead of after school?

• Ask your parents if you can skip family dinner once a week, eating a light meal on your own to make time for a rehersal.

• Reduce hanging out with friends every day after school to twice a week and on Saturdays.

• Try to find a similar group/club that may be less demanding of your time but still allow you to enjoy yourself. If you don't have time for regular yearbook committee meetings, offer to be one of the photographers instead.

• Identify wasted pockets of time (vegging our after school before starting your homework, etc.) and transform them into regular time slots for scheduled activities.

• Maximize your weekend productivity. Although you may think there's nothing better than sleeping in on a Saturday, scheduling an activity such as a sports practice or a class during the morning hours may prove helpful in boosting productivity the rest of the day, maybe even the rest of the weekend.

Special Circumstances:
AFTER-SCHOOL OVERLOAD

Let's face it: Extracurricular activities are not required; they are desired. If your schedule is full of advanced courses *and* you've got several activities crowding your time map, you may have to become selective about which activities you choose to pursue. If friends, teachers, or parents pressure you to take on more than you can carry, figure out what you really want to do and say no to the things you don't. Since many of us are prone to spreading ourselves too thin, you'll probably find that the person you're saying no to most often is yourself.

• Look for balance. For instance, instead of three sports, consider reducing it to one or two, to make room for an artistic or academic pursuit.

• Consider the payoffs. Keep any activity that is helping you achieve multiple goals simultaneously (e.g., not only does that volunteer group look good on your résumé, but it helps you widen your social circle and make a difference in the world).

• Compare workloads. Is one less demanding? Consider cutting any activity that is threatening to monopolize your entire schedule.

• Think about timing. Can this be postponed until next semester or next year?

PHASE 3: ATTACK

It's not easy to keep everything balanced. Once you have set up your after-school activities schedule, there will undoubtedly be distractions that can pull you off course. Unexpected homework assignments and tempting invitations from friends can throw you off balance. If you don't have a way to sort through it all, you risk becoming overinvolved, losing sleep, feeling pulled in a million directions and guilty when your friend begs you for some hangout time but you've got to duck off to another meeting. Extracurricular activities are supposed to make your life more enriching, not more stressful. By applying the WADE formula, you'll learn to stay in balance and feel good about your choices every day.

Jessi Says

Balancing My Schedule

When I switched from dance as a hobby to dance as a full-time commitment, I encountered one of the toughest scheduling challenges ever. For many years, I had danced with a group for five hours every Saturday during the school year and every day over the summer. By the end of my freshman year in high school, I decided that I wanted to become a professional dancer. I checked out a bunch of programs and became fixed on taking eight classes a week.

This was a huge change in my schedule, but I was determined to make it work. The question was: How would I fit in all these classes without sacrificing my performance at school or my general energy level?

For starters, I drew up a time map. Some days I had dance class immediately after school, getting me home by 6:30. Other times, I had hours to kill between school and dance and would get home at 9:00 P.M. On my time map, I entered all my dance classes and then marked the open slots I'd have for doing homework, specifying what kind of work I could do when—depending on how long the break was and whether I'd be home or in transit. I also plotted out times for snacks to make sure I'd keep my energy level up. (All this was color coded, of course.)

When school started, I stuck to my schedule, without any excuses. Once I got into my routine, it not only became second nature but also felt more comfortable than it had been when I had had so much free time on my hands. My performance in school was enhanced because I was happier with what I was doing and felt more balanced between the two important things that I was pursuing in my life. My energy level was even higher. I thought that adding all the dance classes would weigh me down, but it had the opposite effect of boosting my productivity.

STEP 1: WRITE IT DOWN

Once you get involved in a lot of extracurricular activities, there is no getting around the need for a reliable planner, which you must use for 100 percent of your commitments. (See Chapter 7 if you haven't selected a planner yet.)

Record recurring meetings, lessons, and classes directly into your calender. Don't leave it to memory—it's too easy to forget when unexpected work piles on. If your group provides a long-term schedule of games, rehearsals, meetings, or performances, transfer all those dates from their paper printout or Web site into the calendar section of your own planner as soon as you receive the full schedule. This will enable you to see conflicts way in advance, so you will have plenty of time to make decisions about what you are willing to miss, and make the necessary arrangements to have someone fill in for you. Also, when other opportunities and invitations come up (parties, school trips, etc.), having your schedule filled out early prevents double-booking.

Many groups and clubs, however, reschedule meetings and activities frequently, so it's important to adjust your schedule as soon as you receive new information. Unlike school classes, extracurricular activities can vary dramatically. You may work from six to eight one night and five to nine on another. It's important to update your planner consistently if you want to avoid missing anything. With each change of schedule, be sure to record not only the new meeting time but also the adjustments to your homework schedule that are affected by it.

In addition, you need to write down every small assignment and preparation step you have to complete between sessions. Mark them in your planner on the day you plan to do them, or in a master to-do list section, to prevent overscheduling yourself with other obligations.

> "I keep a separate page for each activity in my planner, one for chorus, speech, and yearbook committee, so I know where to look when writing down meeting times and special notes."　　　　　　　　　—Kelly G., 17, California

> "For my senior year of high school, I am living in a firehouse to volunteer as a firefighter/EMT. Keeping track of schoolwork and activities is vital, as you never know when you are going to be dispatched. At the start of each day, I spend about five minutes looking at what activities I have scheduled that day, what's coming up this week, and what tasks I have to accomplish. Performing this review each day keeps me aware of what I have to do and prevents work from piling up until the last minute."　　　　　　　　　—Kyle L., 17, Maryland

💬 "I have a special section in my planner where I write down all my activities." —Benny H., 16, Michigan

STEP 2: ADD IT UP

When it comes to after-school commitments, it's especially easy to miscalculate how long an activity will take. There are so many hidden time costs: travel time, waiting time, extra meetings, off-site activities, fund-raisers, preparation, shopping for supplies. When the time required to complete your to-dos exceeds the time you have available, you wind up with a schedule that does not adequately reflect the reality of your day-to-day life. One task spills over into the time you've allotted for another, creating a chain reaction that takes a heavy toll in the form of sleepless nights and increased anxiety. Only once you've learned how to accurately calculate how long tasks will take can you budget your time properly.

If you need help adding it up, refer to the "Estimating Activities" box. If you're not yet familiar with certain tasks on your list, the best thing to do is to talk to people who have experience in those areas and find out how much time these activities actually take and what they involve. For instance, if you've just joined your school's synchronized-swim group, ask one of the older members to tell you how much time you can expect to spend outside practice every week.

Saxophone Activities

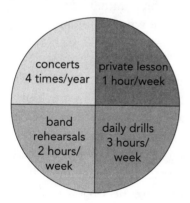

concerts 4 times/year

private lesson 1 hour/week

band rehearsals 2 hours/week

daily drills 3 hours/week

Social Action Committee

phone tree/ e-mail chain 30 mins/week

meetings 2 hours/week (Saturdays)

event planning 3 hours/week

Estimating Activities

See how easy it can be to underestimate.

Activity	Estimated Time	Actual Time
Piano lessons	2 hours/week	Total: 4 hours 45 minutes/week 45-minute lesson 1 time/week 30-minute practice daily 30 minutes/week shopping for sheet music and arranging recital performances
Internship	6 hours/week	Total: 7 hours 30 minutes/week 2 hours of work 3 times/week 30 minutes round-trip 3 times/week

STEP 3: DECIDE WHEN

Most after-school activities are prescheduled. But you will need to decide when you are going to do the preparation related to each activity. Undoubtedly, you will find moments when your plans to prepare conflict with homework, time with friends, plans to prepare for other activities, and your need to just take it easy. Remember resting? When scheduling in your flexible after-school commitments, keep the following in mind:

• **Urgency.** If you have a contact sheet to assemble for the library squad tomorrow and some reading to do for your church meeting on Sunday, get the contact sheet done first to meet your deadline.

• **Priorities.** When there is a conflict between some fund-raising efforts for your community theater group and rehearsing your lines for the play, focus on the task that people are relying on you for most.

• **Satisfaction.** Ask yourself which activity will provide the greatest sense of accomplishment. Is it practicing that song on your guitar or sharpening your argument for that big debate after school?

• **Duration.** If you have only a one-hour window, choose a task (background reading, drafting a meeting agenda, making some phone calls) that will fit the time allotted.

• **Energy level.** Save your peak energy times for SAT prep studying, difficult reading, or paperwork, keeping the fun stuff for when you may be tired. It's usually easier to do things you are passionate about when you are tired, because your love of the activity energizes you.

The Four D's

When there's not enough time and too much to do, it's time to apply the four D's. You have a dance committee meeting and a swim-team practice on the same night. When you're in a bind, here's what you can do.

• **Delete tasks.** Obviously, if you have a direct conflict, you may need to choose one event over another. In this case, you may not necessarily choose to miss the least important. Delete the event that has less meaning to you, or the one you've been doing so well in, you can afford to miss it.

• **Delay tasks.** If you are stuck, see if you can delay a task for a day or even longer. Maybe you can have your fitting for the dance recital this weekend, or gather sponsorships for your marathon in a week, when your schedule calms down a bit.

• **Diminish tasks.** Even though your after-school activities are voluntary, you'd probably feel like you were cheating yourself if you didn't do your absolute best. There are those occasions, however, when there's just no way to get everything done on time. That's when you can start thinking about being more efficient. For example, go to part of the meeting and head straight to the swim meet. Offer to

Jessi Says

D as in Delete

I have a very busy after-school schedule. I not only have dance class and homework every day, but I also fit in other theatrical pursuits (vocal lessons and rehearsals). I'm a participant in a youth movement as well as the camp that is run by it. I periodically volunteer for my old dance troupe, and help out at another dance studio for kids.

A couple of years ago, I volunteered to be the assistant of a director of a small theatrical group. I hoped that I would be able to watch the director at work and see the process of bringing a script to life. I offered to spend my Saturdays at the rehearsals doing whatever was needed, be it holding the script or running out to buy props. Additionally, I'd be given assignments at the end of the rehearsal, such as constructing props, that would have to be completed by the following rehearsal. Some of my time during the week would have to be spent on this job as well.

During the course of the season, I ended up spending a lot more time running errands than being in the theater helping with rehearsals. After the season, despite the fact that my goals had not been completely fulfilled, I decided to go back for another season. I thought that I might be able to help more in the rehearsals themselves the second time around. I was wrong again. I was given even more grunt work and I was completely miserable.

At the end of the season, I decided to quit the position and not replace it in my schedule. Aside from not having a good experience, I felt the pressure of SATs looming in the near future. Freeing up that time would allow me to put more effort into more immediate needs, like starting more intense SAT preparation and just having some time to myself.

come in for an extra rehearsal on the weekend in exchange for leaving a bit earlier the day before a big math test.

• **Delegate tasks.** Now it's time to get creative. If you can't attend a meeting, send your notes to the committee members via e-mail and ask a friend who is attending to take notes for you. If you're organizing a bake sale and don't have time to bake anything, offer to swap responsibilities with another group member, taking on the role of cashier instead. (Or delegate the baking to Sara Lee. As long as you raise money, it doesn't have to be your best brownies this time.)

STEP 4: EXECUTE YOUR PLAN

It all seems fairly easy so far, right? Not so fast—when it comes to executing your plan, you'll need to be on the lookout for the three culprits before you can reward yourself for your victories.

Culprit #1: Interruptions

Sometimes, even the best-laid after-school plans get interrupted by demands from other areas of your life: friends and family who want your time, an extra-big homework load. It's up to you to fulfill your commitments and set the tone of seriousness. Periodically, you can allow something to keep you from completing your responsibilities but, for the most part, stick to your commitments. You'll feel much more fulfilled.

Meetings, rehearsals, and practices sometimes disrupt your plans by going longer than planned because of interruptions of their own. People show up late; meetings go off on tangents; teachers and leaders may want to keep you longer to master a particular skill.

You can also interrupt your own plans by giving in to the temptation to let an activity carry on past its allotted time frame. You need to be disciplined. If friends want to grab a quick bite after play rehearsal, you may have to decline the invite and rush home to make it to your other activities. If student council meetings tend to run late, you can inform the activity leader of your previous commitments in advance and ask that you be allowed to finish up your business and leave early.

> **Minimizing Interruptions**
> - Create a meeting agenda to keep the group on track.
> - Work extra time into your schedule for sudden interruptions.

Culprit #2: Procrastination and Lateness

Usually people procrastinate about doing their after-school activities because they don't get as much enjoyment out of them as they used to or thought they would. Or they procrastinate about the things that are harder or more tedious to do (practicing an instrument, learning lines, studying for the college prep exam). Establish a regular time to tackle the hard work—preferably during your peak energy times or when you are stuck somewhere and have no other distractions. One teen did his college prep on the long bus ride to school, guaranteeing thirty minutes of study time each day. Schedule just enough time to complete the task, and make sure you have a fun activity planned on the other side of it to reward yourself.

Culprit #3: Perfectionism

Although excellence is a worthy goal, if it means that you're going to get overinvolved in your activities, perfectionism can stand in the way of your peace of mind. For instance, just because you enjoy writing for the school paper doesn't necessarily mean that you need to be editor in chief, a position that might force you to neglect a lot of your other activities as well as your schoolwork. If you are in a community group, you don't have to volunteer for every committee—bite off only as much as you can truly deliver on. Pace yourself with your after-school involvements to maintain balance and sanity in your life.

Reward Yourself

Making the time to participate in activities that have absolutely nothing to do with graduating from high school is a big accomplishment in and of itself. Don't forget to reward yourself for your efforts. Whether it's winning a tennis match, getting a high five from your drama teacher, or simply completing a semester of tuba lessons, make sure you take yourself out for a celebration and do something you enjoy. Make a habit of rewarding yourself. After all, you deserve it!

10

Social Life

Project Checklist	
MATERIALS	Planner Time map Priorities
ESTIMATED TIME	1–2 hours

Staying active socially can be pivotal to a teen's happiness, and with good reason: building solid and supportive friendships, dating, and spending time with our families can make us feel good about ourselves and teach us a lot about who we are and who we want to be.

Finding time for a social life isn't always easy, especially for those teens who are very academically or extracurricularly oriented. On the other hand, preventing social activities from monopolizing one's schedule can also present a formidable challenge for those teens who are attempting to date and maintain a large number of friendships. It's a matter of striking a balance. This chapter will offer ways to enjoy a satisfying social life and still find time for other important matters like school, extracurricular activities, and some good old-fashioned private time.

PHASE 1: ANALYZE

If you've developed a reputation for always bailing out on plans at the last minute, or if your social life has swallowed up your entire schedule and you find yourself with little time for school and anything else, it's time to address the following four questions.

Question #1: What's Working and What's Not?

Be brutally honest as you identify what in your social life needs work and what's just fine as is. To give you an idea, here are what some other teens had to say on the subject.

What's Working?

 "I get together with my camp friends at least once a month." —Aidan B., 17, Massachusetts

"I stay in touch with all my friends on-line." —Hannah G., 13, California

"I enjoy hanging out with my family on Sundays." —Marci W., 16, Kansas

What's Not?

 "I don't have enough time to spend with my friends."

—Jenny C., 16, Maryland

"I always have to cancel at the last minute because I double-book my friends and family events." —Chris S., 15, Georgia

"My friends call when I am in the middle of my homework." —Bobby D., 16, Colorado

To analyze what's working and what's not, evaluate each area of your social life or each person you spend time with according to the following criteria.

• Enjoyment. Do you have fun together? Is the time you spend with this person or activity relaxing and pleasant or uncomfortable and strained? Do you look forward to get-togethers? Do you feel happier afterward?

• Compatibility. Do you share values and ethics or do you disagree about what's right and wrong? Do you enjoy similar kinds of activities? Do you have schedules that are compatible or are you never available at the same time?

• Supportiveness. Does this person make you feel good about yourself? Does this person accept you for who you are or is this person pressuring you to be someone you are not? Do you feel loved and cared about or disregarded and unimportant? Can you go to this person for advice that you value?

Use the following example to guide you.

Friends	_____ Enjoyment
	_____ Compatibility
	_____ Supportiveness
	_____ Other:
Family	_____ Enjoyment
	_____ Compatibility
	_____ Supportiveness
	_____ Other:
Dating	_____ Enjoyment
	_____ Compatibility
	_____ Supportiveness
	_____ Other:

OR

Laura	_____ Enjoyment _____ Compatibility _____ Supportiveness _____ Other:
Rob	_____ Enjoyment _____ Compatibility _____ Supportiveness _____ Other:
Beth	_____ Enjoyment _____ Compatibility _____ Supportiveness _____ Other:

Now that you've got your completed survey in front of you, you can start identifying the major problems. Is the time you spend with your boy/girlfriend taking away from your friendships? Are you blowing off family, friends, and romance to focus solely on school-related activities? This survey will help you figure out where and how your social life is out of balance so that you can begin working out possible solutions.

Question #2: What's Your Essential 7?

Social lives come in all shapes and sizes. Some of us bond via computer, others by phone, and still others in person. To identify how your social life operates, you need to consider all of your social outlets, planning tools, and personal habits. Your Essential 7 here could be either a list of the optimal conditions or attitudes you believe are key to a smoothly running social life, or the specific items you may need to coordinate your social activities. To get you on your way, we've compiled an Essential 7 list for two teens, one of which is more attitude-based, the other more pragmatic.

Social Life Essentials for Adam K., 13

1. Bike
2. E-mail/IM
3. Phone
4. Allowance
5. Weekend free time
6. Parent driver
7. Parents' permission

Social Life Essentials for Jena D., 18

1. Knowing what I need to do for my own happiness
2. Not losing contact with people I have fun with
3. Keeping a general positive vibe
4. Keeping communication open, especially when there is a misunder-standing
5. Reflecting and reevaluating my social needs periodically
6. Maintaining perspective—remembering this is a small period in my life and not getting caught up in drama
7. Refusing to let other people bring me down

💬 "I leave Saturdays clear for social time, and make sure to plan in advance."
—Sam M., 17, Vermont

💬 "I set aside one hour of phone time each night to return my friends' calls."
—Lee L., 13, New York

💬 "My boyfriend and I limit our phone calls during weeknights."
—Amanda T., 16, Illinois

Question #3: What's the Payoff?

Fun is one of the major payoffs of social life, but it's far from the only one. Our friends, families, and boy/girlfriends make us feel accepted and connected, they help us snap out of our not-so-happy moments, they enrich our lives with their different viewpoints and personalities, and, of course, they're fun to hang out with. Friends can also help us in other areas of our lives, like school and after-school activities.

What does your social life do for you? How does spending time with your friends and family help you achieve your big-picture goals? Is there anything you would like to change about your social life? Are you satisfied with all your current relationships?

> "I'd like to make new friends outside my current social circle."   —Peter W., 18, Connecticut

Jessi Says

Finding Balance

Being very goal driven, I tend to fill my schedule to the brim with academic and extracurricular activities. The downside of this ambitious work regimen is that it often leaves very little time for getting together with my friends.

When I first began to pile on the work, I didn't really think twice about the consequences a lack of social time might have. My friends are very supportive and our relationships are solid. I wasn't concerned about the possibility of losing friends because I knew they'd be understanding of my new commitments. I still saw and spoke to them in school and went to lunch, but after school I went straight to dance class and stayed until late, and come Friday and Saturday nights, I was at home hitting the books or developing some new project to work on. Phone conversations were quick and short, usually about tests or homework.

As time passed, however, I began to feel very dreary and fried from all the work. Not because I wasn't enjoying it, but because I was pouring all my energy into the same things over and over, and never stopping to refresh myself. Soon it was time for winter break, and my school friends and I had a holiday gift-exchange party. I had so much fun just being relaxed and hanging out again, and I left the party feeling incredibly rejuvenated. I realized how important it was for me to spend time with my friends to regain some balance in my life and perspective on my work. I made a new resolution to do something purely social at least once every two weeks, if not once a week, and I've done my best to stick to it. It's paid off: Not only does seeing my friends fill me with new energy, but it makes me a happier person in general.

💬 "I want to balance the pressure and stress of school with more time off to relax and enjoy myself."
                                        –Dana B., 16, Washington

💬 "I want to feel connected to my family by spending time with them."   –Fiona O., 15, Florida

💬 "I need to balance quality time with my girlfriend without sacrificing my grades."   –Mihkel S., 17, New York

Question #4: What's the Problem?

There are a variety of obstacles that can stand between you and an organized social life. It may be that you just transferred schools and all your friends are far away. Maybe your friends call and keep you on the phone for hours. It could be that you're spreading yourself too thin with school, a job, and extracurriculars. All your time might be spent on taking care of your younger siblings. Or it could be that your confidence is in need of a boost. The point is that there are countless problems that can get in the way.

Some of the most common reasons for a disorganized social life are listed below. Check all those that apply.

❑ In transition	❑ More tasks than time	❑ Lack of confidence
❑ Poor time estimation	❑ Limited mobility	❑ Conflicting schedules
❑ Competing social groups	❑ Conflicting values	❑ Parental restrictions

PHASE 2: STRATEGIZE

Now that you've analyzed your social calendar, you're aware of the various groups, activities, and individuals involved and how they fit or don't fit into your overall schedule. You're one step closer to the balanced lifestyle you want. It's time to start thinking about how you can better arrange your social life to suit your needs and goals.

Julie's Work Journal:

Aaron's Story

Aaron and Robbie went to different schools in the same town. They had met through their parents, who were good friends, and ended up becoming really close themselves. When they were younger, they got together whenever the families did. But by the time they hit junior high school, life had gotten more complicated. Each was involved in his own academic and extracurricular life, and since one was in private and the other in public school, their vacation schedules didn't even match. For a while, Aaron wasn't sure if Robbie was still interested in their friendship, and Robbie was secretly worried about the same thing. When their families got together for a barbecue one summer, the boys realized how much they missed each other. The problem here was simple: They had conflicting schedules and they were spending less time at family gatherings. They needed to make plans *on their own* if they wanted to see each other.

I suggested that they make a commitment to get together every couple of months—seeing a movie, going to a basketball game, or going roller blading. They had to make these plans way in advance and be willing to arrange transportation on their own. Though it took some effort, they were both motivated to follow through because each of them appreciated having a close friend outside of their main social group.

Adjust Your Time Map

If you've been following Part 3 from the beginning, your time map should already include your academic and after-school responsibilities. If you're reading this chapter individually, take a moment to go back to Chapter 7 to get a quick overview of how to create a time map.

Once you have filled in your school and extracurricular commitments, take a good look at how many time slots are left over for social activities. In light of what you learned during the "Analyze" section of this chapter, do you think there is too little time left over for your social life? Too much? Are you clear on what kind of social activity you'll be doing during any given time slot? For instance, will you be reserving Saturday or Sunday mornings for attending religious services with your family? Will Friday nights be reserved for friends? Will lunch breaks be used for studying or socializing, or a clever combination of the two? If there's anything that needs changing or clarifying, now's the time.

Questions to Ask Yourself

- How many social activities can my schedule accommodate?
- How much social interaction do I need each week/month to feel comfortable?
- Can I cut back on any extracurricular activities to make more time for a social life?
- Are there any ways to combine social life with after-school activities or academics (e.g., study group)?
- Is my social life interfering with school? Is school interfering with my social life?
- Would I rather reserve my social activity for the weekends or space it out evenly throughout the week?
- Do I prefer to plan ahead or be spontaneous about my social activities?

PHASE 3: ATTACK

You've set aside time for your social life, dividing it between family, friends, and maybe dating. Even if you've decided to keep your social time a little flexible, you still need to be very organized to make sure people and plans don't slip through the cracks. How do you juggle the invitations, phone calls, get-togethers, and spontaneous moments? You got it: by applying the WADE formula.

STEP 1: WRITE IT DOWN

Everything–from placing a phone call to making plans for the weekend, from formal dinner parties with your parents to informal get-togethers with friends–needs to be entered into your planner. If your family is going on vacation, write it down–including the packing time. If you are planning a surprise party for a friend, make a list of each task you will need to do to make it happen–from addressing the invitations to baking the cake.

Use the calendar section of your planner to record dates and

Special Circumstances:
IN TRANSITION

Moved to a new town? Just graduated from middle school? Starting over is never easy, no matter how old you are. If you find yourself in transition, understand that feeling lonely is completely normal. We've all been there. What's challenging is the fact that you need to spend extra time developing new friends, while at the same time trying to learn your way around a new place and keep up in school.

One way to jump-start your social life is to focus on finding one friend first instead of trying to connect to a whole group. One friend can lead to other introductions and can keep you from feeling down while you're in transition. And be sure to stay in touch with your old friends by phone, e-mail, or letters. Knowing there are people who love you can give you the confidence to make new friends.

Armed with an adjusted time map, you should have a clearer idea about the strategies you'll need to take to improve and balance your social life. Read on to find out how to translate your strategies into action.

events. Use the daily section for to-do items: specific phone calls you want to make, letters you want to write, family activities you want to do. For example, if you've set aside Saturday mornings for letter writing, indicate which letters you are going to write on which day. If you're not sure about certain plans, mark them in pencil. This way, if a conflicting invitation comes up, you will know that you had tentative plans and can make a fully informed decision. (Double-booking is a big danger if you don't record *all* events in your planner.)

What about contact information like phone numbers, addresses, and e-mail accounts? Is all this information clearly organized? Your planner should include a section for important numbers. Consider recording the information alphabetically by first or last name (whichever way your mind works). When getting new contact information from a friend, take a few extra seconds to ask about and record everything at once: e-mail address, street address, zip code, home phone, cell phone, and parents' phone numbers if different. Some people choose not to use their planner for contact information. Instead, they have a running list posted on the wall of their room, or they use the auto-dial of their cell phones for important numbers. But if you use the cell-phone approach, make sure you have the numbers written down at home, too, in case you lose your phone.

 *Back It Up!*

If you use an electronic planner, never forget the importance of backing up all your contact information for friends and family on your hard drive. No matter how sophisticated, technology can go haywire from time to time. To avoid losing all your important data, hotsync at the same time every day.

STEP 2: ADD IT UP

Social activities are not like classes, which have a set beginning and end time. You probably know all too well that because of their informal and unstructured nature, social activities can go on much longer than anticipated. For instance, you'll call your friend, thinking you'll chat for ten minutes. Next thing you know, you've spent more than an hour on the phone. Or you think you'll take one minute to write a quick e-mail, when it actually takes you about fifteen minutes. Or you've showed up on time to meet your friend at the movies, but she's nowhere to be found and finally shows up half an hour late. Even movies, which usually don't run longer than two hours, can wind up taking a lot more time if you're always agreeing to grab a bite to eat afterward. That's why it's so important to be realistic when calculating the time your social activities take up.

However, being realistic doesn't mean forgoing your plans. It simply means you'll have to learn to set your own boundaries. Social activities are not all-or-nothing propositions. You can still go out to lunch on Saturday; just make sure that what you scheduled as a one-hour meal doesn't turn into an all-day extravaganza. And don't forget the importance of building in cushion time when estimating how long activities will take. If you know your boy/girlfriend has a habit of showing up late, make sure to build an extra twenty minutes into those activities.

If you need help in the adding-it-up department, refer to the "Estimates versus Actual Times" box, on page 206.

STEP 3: DECIDE WHEN

The best thing about social activities is that you're in control. Of course, you can't tell someone when to throw their party or to sit by the phone in case you call, but you can decide how long to stay at a party and how long to continue your phone conversation. You can also decide when to IM or call your friends, and you're ultimately responsible for how much time you spend with your family after you get home from school.

When you're assigning homes and deciding what to do when, use the following factors to help guide your decisions:

• **Urgency.** There shouldn't be too many situations where urgency is the deciding force in your social life. However, if you have a friend who is visiting from out of town for a brief stay, making time to get together may take priority. Or, if a friend or family member is going through a crisis and needs your help, chances are you'll want to be there for him or her. If a friend is *always* in crisis, however, you may need to reconsider his or her constant requests for attention.

• **Variety.** While you may not realize it, your social life can benefit greatly from an occasional change of pace. Finding new, fun, and unique activities can help keep things from getting boring. Try something uncharacteristic—go to a play, car or electronics show, or plan a theme party. Variety can also apply to the people you hang out with. While having a core best friend or core group you spend much of your time with is comforting and fun, expanding your social circle can keep your horizons broad, expose you to some new ideas, and make you feel a little less dependent on your group if they end up doing things that upset you from time to time. It's all about balance.

• **Significance.** When deciding what to do and with whom, choose those activities and people that will support and enhance your big-picture goals. If one of your friends is always pressuring you to do something you don't enjoy, try to limit your interaction or allot that friend less time in your schedule. It's important to be true to yourself so that your social life is an extension of rather than a detraction from your personal interests.

Estimates versus Actual Times

The following examples should give you some idea of how easy it is to under-estimate the time social activities actually take up. Use these samples as a guideline in making your own calculations.

Social Activity	Estimated Time	Actual Time
Friends	10 hours/week	Total: 14 hours 30 minutes 50-minute lunch 5 times/week 1 hour after school 50-minute free period 5 hours 1 night/week 30 minutes phone 7 times/week
Family	6 hours/week	Total: 12 hours 1-hour dinners 6 times/week 4-hour outing on Sundays 2-hour religious services

• **Duration.** Decide how long each activity will take. Figure in prep time, travel time, and waiting-for-friends-to-show-up time, and schedule accordingly. When in doubt, tack on twenty minutes as a cushion.

• **Energy or interest level.** Some friends and events are so comfortable and enjoyable, they actually give you energy, so it doesn't matter how tired you are when you get together. Others require more effort, so be sure to check your energy level before saying yes. Also, consider how interested you are in the proposed activity. For instance, if your friends like to go to the movies on weekends but you're not too crazy about the ones you've been seeing together lately, you can beg off the next time around.

The Four D's

It's all too easy (and tempting) to imagine a world in which your social life monopolizes your schedule. When you can't fit it all in, put the four D's to work.

• **Delete tasks.** Saying no is a valuable skill, so you may as well perfect this art while you're still young. If your schedule is bursting at the seams with social activities, you can start cutting the fat right now. Social life shouldn't be a pressure cooker; it should *relieve* pressure. So say no to anything that you're not gung ho about . . . and that includes those nightly conversations with a certain friend who never seems to run out of problems to talk about. You should also consider distancing yourself from friends who drain you of your energy or monopolize all your time without giving anything back. Spend more time with friends who understand the art of give-and-take. Finally, make a list of all your social activities. Go through the list, one activity at a time, and ask yourself: Does this activity fit in with my big-picture goals? Does this friend support me or make me feel bad about myself? Delete anything that doesn't fuel you.

• **Delay tasks.** If a friend wants to get together at a time you are unavailable, you don't necessarily have to say no. You can always take a rain check. Propose a different day or time for getting together (or completing that phone call). As long as you live up to your commitment, everyone will be happy. Don't forget, it's up to you to control your social life. It's important not to let friends or boy/girlfriends determine how you spend your time.

• **Diminish tasks.** All too often, social life becomes all about making everyone else happy when it should be about making ourselves happy. That's why diminishing can be so effective . . . it's about separating your needs and what you want to do from the needs and wants of your friends, family, and boy/girlfriend. For example, if the night's plans call for pizza and a movie, but you have a ton of work to do, bow out of the movie and meet up for pizza. If your friends are all getting together for an overnight retreat, but you can't possibly spend a whole weekend away, help them pack or see them off at the bus station. Or, if you know your friend will spend an hour talking about her new crush, ask her/him to e-mail or IM you instead. Trying to

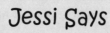

Jessi Says

Staying Connected

Having changed schools, gone to camp, and met a lot of people through dance, I have built many circles of friends. These different groups require varying levels and degrees of attention and nurturing.

I'll start with my close group of friends from school. Because we have the advantage of seeing each other for six hours a day, five days a week, staying in touch is a cinch. We rely on each other for someone to sit with at lunch and get the homework assignment from when we are absent. We can presume that something will be happening with some variation of our groups on Friday and Saturday nights, and we can more often than not assume ourselves invited.

I performed with the same dance troupe for thirteen years, graduating at the end of my freshman year of high school. Maintaining the relationships with the people from this group is a greater challenge because seeing them always requires making plans. I talk to several people from the troupe occasionally, but we generally rely on e-mail for communicating. The alumni put together an annual production that provides an automatic time for catch-up.

Communicating with my friends from camp is very different. Our camp holds many get-togethers throughout the year. But I can't go to a lot of these because of my dance schedule. Many of us do communicate on a daily basis through a service called mass mail, which automatically forwards any correspondence we write to all of the members of our group at once. We communicate about all kinds of things—from a detailed account of someone's day, to political disputes, to general questions for everyone to contribute to. There can be anywhere from one to more than a hundred e-mails on any given day. When we actually want to get together (casually, as opposed to camp-arranged gatherings), the goal is to have everyone there. This requires two things: a date that works for the majority, and a house with nice parents who don't mind thirty-some-odd kids sleeping on any horizontal surface they can find. It's not easy to satisfy these two requirements.

To me, keeping all the friends that I have been lucky enough to acquire over the years is important, and so I do my best to give every friendship what it needs.

answer all your e-mails in one sitting and in a preset amount of time can also help keep your schedule under control.

• **Delegate.** If you have a group of friends, no matter how small, delegating can be easy. When one friend needs more attention than you alone can deliver, simply call on your mutual friends and ask that they pitch in to help this friend in need. Also, if you've made plans with a friend but can't make it that day, you can suggest that a mutual friend take your place. As long as you don't make a habit of this, your friends will appreciate your efforts to meet your obligations.

STEP 4: EXECUTE YOUR PLAN

When it comes to executing your plan, watch out for the following three culprits and don't forget to reward yourself each time your attempts meet with success.

Culprit #1: Frequent Interruptions

Minimizing interruptions and their impact is easier said than done when it comes to dealing with friends. How many times have you scheduled to hang out with a friend, only to be interrupted by another friend who just can't wait to spill the latest gossip? If you find yourself being pulled from every direction by competing friendships, make sure to focus your energy on each friend one at a time so they can feel that you really care about them. Make sure the time you spend together is all about quality. Listen to your friends and let them know you're there for them.

Culprit #2: Procrastination and Lateness

Procrastination and lateness can cause a lot of problems in your social life. Procrastination often occurs when you are less than enthusiastic about the activity you are doing or the people with whom you are getting together. If that's the case, be honest with yourself and simply bow out of the invitation. There's no sense torturing yourself or the group if you don't want to be there.

As for lateness, some people thrive on the adrenaline rush that comes with trying to beat the clock. If you like to rush around like a chicken with its head cut off, keep in mind that it's not fair to keep your friends waiting: They have taken time out of their busy schedules to enjoy their time off with you. Try setting aside more time for preparation. Or set your clock fifteen minutes early so you can arrive on time. If your friends are the ones who are always running behind, try explaining that their lateness is inconsiderate because it shortens the time you have set aside to enjoy their company. Even if they don't mend their ways, chronic latecomers don't have to throw you off track. If you know that certain friends are always late, you can tell them to meet you a half hour ahead of the scheduled time.

Culprit #3: Perfectionism

Everyone knows that you can't please all the people all the time, so don't break your back trying. Make sure not to overschedule activities, be selective about accepting invitations, and don't bow to the pressure of being popular or dating. If you're not ready for romance yet, that's fine—you have your entire life. And if you prefer the company of one or two friends to a large group, don't try to live up to other people's expectations by neglecting your own needs. Remember, the closest you can get to perfection is to be happy and satisfied with yourself.

Reward Yourself

Making positive choices and finding time for your social life is a reward in and of itself. It provides you with companions, fun, support, and a sense of belonging. Recognize every achievement, whether it be withstanding peer pressure and declining an invite or actually finding the time to hang out with your friends because of some proactive planning on your part. Then reward yourself by focusing on the moment and putting aside thoughts of homework or other obligations. The key to getting the most out of your social life is to carve out the time, choose your friends wisely, and enjoy!

To Parents and Teachers

When I was a teen, I was notoriously disorganized. My bedroom was always so cluttered with clothes, papers, books, and junk that you could never see the actual floor. Very few items on my to-do list ever got done, either because I procrastinated getting started or I forgot they had to be done in the first place. I was late for practically everything, from school to dinner to airplane flights.

My parents and teachers were understandably exasperated. They pleaded, begged, and scolded me often—stressing that my disorganized ways were keeping me from fulfilling my potential and were creating problems for all those around me. Like most teens, if I felt I was being lectured to or ordered to do something, I rebelled. And the truth was, no one was suggesting *how* to get organized—they were simply pointing out that it was necessary . . . and I was pretty clueless as to how to proceed.

It was only when my own daughter was born that I finally experienced a breakthrough. One day after spending over two frenetic hours getting ready to take her for a walk, I realized that Jessi would never see the light of day if I didn't get my act together. Starting with the diaper bag, I organized my life in incremental stages over the next couple of years. Having finally mastered the skill, I became a professional organizer in 1989. Nine years later I wrote the *New York Times* best-seller *Organizing from the Inside Out* and then *Time Management from the Inside Out*, both of which teach readers how to custom-design their organizing systems based on the unique way they think and on their natural habits and goals.

The idea for *Organizing from the Inside Out for Teens* came to me when Jessi was in seventh grade. Her English teacher had asked me to come in and talk to the class about the experience of writing a book. I'd carefully prepared my presentation to cover such topics as overcoming writer's block, organizing your chapters and materials, and dealing with publishers. I was taken aback to find that 75 percent of the questions from the kids were focused on organizing and time management, and not necessarily in relation to book writing but to their lives as a whole.

Teens today really *want* to be on top of things. They are under enormous pressure to do well in school, build a college résumé, have an active extracurricular schedule, maintain a social life, perform well on PSATs, SATSs, AP classes . . . the list goes on and on.

Struggles between adults and teens about getting organized are common but, I think, altogether unnecessary. If you begin with the premise that every teen wants to do well and succeed, there is no need for conflict. Organizing and time management are vehicles for self-expression and self-discovery. And that's what being a teen is all about. Rather than lecture or teach, your role is to coach and guide. Mastering the skills of organization can actually offer a means by which the two of you can build a relationship, or strengthen an already existing one.

Organizing from the Inside Out for Teens is based on the same philosophies and strategies introduced in my first two books, but adapted for the unique stage of life teens are in. Teens are still discovering themselves, and are not necessarily clear on their life goals. Their priorities and interests change frequently. They have less control over their environments and schedules than adults. *Organizing from the Inside Out for Teens* is more visual and interactive, with self-tests and quizzes. There is new material created especially for teens.

The book is written directly to teens, but this doesn't mean there isn't room for adult involvement. The degree of involvement will almost certainly vary from parent to parent, teacher to teacher. You might simply give them the book (or leave it lying around), and allow them to tackle the process on their own, while you watch unobtrusively (and noncritically) from the sidelines. Or you could play a more active role, offering to be available for support, companionship, and/or guidance along the way. If you don't have organizing skills of your own, you can learn alongside your teen—using their room/space/schedule as the learning laboratory. If you do have organizing skills, avoid advocating your own organizing system as the only or best way. The following strategies will help ensure that your experience in helping your teen get organized brings both of you closer together instead of into conflict:

1. Make sure you've read the book. If you are short on time, cover at least the first two chapters and then skip to the chapter for the area you and your teen are about to organize.

2. Build your teen's confidence. Eliminate phrases such as, "You are so disorganized!" "You are such a slob." "Clean your room—it's a pigsty!" "Stop procrastinating or you'll never make it through school!" Everybody is organized in some ways. Identify and recognize the way in which your teen is organized and repeat it to them consistently and confidently.

3. Respect their ways of thinking and their goals and attachments. You might group shirts by short- and long-sleeve—your teen might prefer to group by fabric weight or style. You might be a morning person while your teen is a night owl. As long as their system works for *them*, support it.

4. Eliminate prejudgments. You can't tell whether a person is organized or not by looking at a space. Ask what works for them and what doesn't. You may be surprised what you learn.

5. Reinforce their commitment. If your teen gets overwhelmed or discouraged, ask him or her to rearticulate the reasons for wanting to get organized. (Remember, teens must get organized for their own reasons—not just to please you. What are *they* trying to get out of it?) Empathize when your teen gets frustrated. Don't automatically jump to solving the problem—express your confidence that your teen can and will find what works for him or her.

6. Act as a sounding board, but let them decide. Do not impose your opinions. This is a rare opportunity to learn how teens think, to share their goals and dreams, to discover what's truly important to them.

7. Make the project easier on them physically. There are so many ways you can help carry out their master plan—gathering containers, purchasing planners, tying up filled trash bags, helping with labeling, transporting giveaways, returning unearthed objects that belong elsewhere in the house back to their original homes.

8. Help keep them focused from "the inside out." If your teen asks "should" questions (Where should I put this? How should I categorize this? Should I throw this out?), throw the question back by asking "What do you think? What are your instincts telling you?" If you do share your opinion, always preface your remarks by saying, "Well, what would work for me is . . . But you may find a better way for you."

9. Pace them. Encourage your teen to focus on one chapter at a time, completing one area before moving on to the next.

Don't expect instant results—becoming organized is a process, mastered and refined over a lifetime. But do remember that organizing and time management are life skills (not talents) that *can* be learned. You can facilitate your teen's mastery of these life skills . . . even if you never learned to get organized yourself. Read this book alongside your teen—it may help you organize your own life!

Happy organizing,
Julie

Sources for Organizing Containers

Exposures Photo Supplies	(800) 572-5750	www.exposuresonline.com
Get Organized	(800) 803-9400	www.getorg-inc.com
Hold Everything	(800) 421-2264	www.williams-sonomainc.com
Ikea	(800) 434-4532	www.ikea.com
Lillian Vernon	(800) 285-5555	www.lillianvernon.com
Organization Etc.	(877) 674-2649	www.organizationetc.com
Pottery Barn	(800) 922-5507	www.potterybarn.com
Red Envelope	(877) 733-3683	www.redenvelope.com
Reliable Home Office	(800) 869-6000	www.reliable.com
Sephora	(877) SEPHORA	www.sephora.com
Stacks and Stacks	(877) 278-2257	www.stacksandstacks.com
The Container Store	(800) 733-3532	www.thecontainerstore.com
Urban Outfitters	(800) 282-2200	www.urbanoutfitters.com

Retail Chains that Carry Organizing Products

Barnes & Noble		www.barnesandnoble.com
Bed, Bath & Beyond	(800) GO BEYOND	www.bedbathandbeyond.com
Home Depot	1-800-430-3376	www.homedepot.com
K-mart	(866) KMART4U	www.bluelight.com
Marshalls	(888) MARSHALLS	www.marshallsonline.com
Office Depot	(888) GO-DEPOT	www.officedepot.com
Office Max	(800) 283-7674	www.officemax.com
Staples	(800) 3-STAPLE	www.staples.com
Target	(800) 440-0680	www.target.com
TJ Maxx	(800) 926-6299	www.tjmaxx.comm
Wal-mart	(800) WAL-MART	www.walmart.com

Bags

Case Logic	(877) 227-3347	www.caselogic.com
Eagle Creek	(800) 874-1048	www.eaglecreek.com
Fossil	(800) 449-3056	www.fossil.com
Hobo	(800) 277-HOBO	corporateoffice@hobobags.com
L. L. Bean	(800) 441-5713	www.llbean.com
Manhattan Portage		www.manhattanportage.com
Walker Bags		www.walkerbags.com
Yak Pak	(800) 292-5725	www.yakpak.com

Brands with Teen-Friendly Product Lines

Eldon		www.eldonsolutions.com
Esselte		www.esselte.com
Smead	(651) 437-4111	www.smead.com

Retail Chains that Carry Planners

Barnes & Noble		www.barnesandnoble.com
K-mart	(866) KMART4U	www.bluelight.com
Office Depot	(888) GO-DEPOT	www.officedepot.com
office Max	(800) 383-7674	www.officemax.com
Staples	(800 3-STAPLE	www.staples.com
Target	(800) 440-0680	www.target.com
Wal-mart	(800) WAL-MART	www.walmart.com

Digital Planners

Handspring		www.handspring.com
Palm Pilot		www.palm.com
Handango.com		www.handango.com

Time-Management Products

Levenger	(800) 544-0880	www.levenger.com
The Daily Planner	(800) 635-4321	www.thedailyplanner.com
Filofax		www.filofax.com
Mead/At-a-Glance	(800) 323-0500	www.mead.com
Day Runner	(800) 232-9786	www.dayrunner.com
Day Timer	(800) 225-5005	www.daytimer.com
Franklin-Covey	(800) 842-2439	www.franklin-covey.com
Time Wise	(800) 523-8060	

ACKNOWLEDGMENTS

Julie's

The process of writing this book was a pure pleasure, because of the tremendous talents and incredible teamwork of a wonderful group of people.

First and foremost, eternal thanks to my agent Joni Evans for coming into my life and gracing it with such wisdom, strength, vision, and limitless support. You've shown me how to create and rely on a team, and I'm so deeply grateful you're part of mine.

To Jessi, my coauthor. Collaborating with you was a true joy—your professionalism, commitment, insights, and contributions fueled me, inspired me, and enriched each and every page with truth. So proud of you, so grateful to you, and so very honored to be your mom.

To Elina Furman, whose hand on the structure and assembly of this book kept us moving at a steady and productive pace and allowed us to focus on content, nuance, and details in a way that made this book the best it could be. Thank you for your incredible energy, enthusiasm, and skill.

To Jennifer Barth, our editor, whose keen eye, vivid imagination, and fantastic time-management skills brought this book to a brilliant shine. Your understanding of the reader, respect for each person's contributions, and compassionate guidance were a delight.

To Faith Hamlin and Peter McGuigan of Sanford J. Greenberger and Associates, most heartfelt gratitude for helping me establish such a solid foundation to my writing career, and for your continual support as I grow.

Deepest appreciation to John Sterling at Holt, for believing in this book and the importance of the subject. Continuous thanks to Maggie Richards, Elizabeth Shreve, Sarah Hutson, Ruth Kaplan, and David Sobel for your practical support, many ideas, and full backing on each of our projects. My most enduring, heartfelt thank you to Tracey Locke for being there on September 11—waiting for Jessi and bringing her across the bridge to me.

I feel so fortunate to have been embraced by the incredible team at William Morris Agency, who provide me with a steady stream of expertise, guidance, and support. A huge thank you to Joni's assistant Andy McNichol, Glenn Gulino and his assistant Al Trombetta, Lisa Shotland, Kenneth Slotnik, Eric Zohn, Brian Dubin, Jim Ornstein, and Alan Trombeto. The day I signed the Big Book was one of the most exciting in my career. I know I couldn't be in better hands.

To Oprah, I extend my deepest appreciation for creating a universal culture which challenges us all to live our best lives, do our best work, be our best selves. It is an honor to contribute to that vision, and a pure joy to participate in the journey.

Immeasurable gratitude and the hugest of hugs to Amy Gross, Gayle King, Pat Towers, Lisa Kogan, Sudie Redmond, JJ Miller, Tari Ayala, and the staff at *O Magazine*—for welcoming me to the fold, for sharing your wisdom and talents, and for setting a standard of excellence that has lifted my writing and thinking to new heights. I learn so much from each of you every day.

To all of the folks at the *Oprah Winfrey Show* who have placed such trust in me—Diane, Ellen, Lisa E, Angie K, Caroline Z, Chelsea M, Andrea W, Jill V, Heather A, Mollie A, Leisa M, Lisa M, Jack M, Terry G. I'm honored to be part of the family and deeply appreciate your extraordinary talent at bringing such powerful concepts and learning to television.

Joe Garbarino at Twin Cities Public Television has served as visionary, advocate, protector, and angel to my career. Your call on September 11 meant the world to me. Thanks also to Gerry Richman, Erikka Herman, and Wendy Graham for your guidance and support. To Danny Levin and Reid Tracy at Hay House for your enthusiasm, integrity, and humanity.

I could not write or perform as I do without the support of my devoted team at TASK MASTERS. To Anna Hicks, Kara Brickman, Stephen Ott, Alexandra Merino, Mary Jo McConnell, Ellen Kosloff, and Cloe Axelson. Thank you for keeping the business going while I ducked into the writing hole for hours, and sometimes days, on end. A special thanks to Anna Sutherland for transcribing my scribbled brainstorms into text, and reviewing my work when I got stuck. To

Ron Young, for so many years of friendship and support, and Deb Kinney for keeping the clients happy.

Many, many thanks to our growing team of TASK MASTERS Organizers for embracing the vision and spreading the power of organizing from the inside out nationwide: Sue Becker, Anita Berg, Karen Denton-Betts, Janna Hartwell, Tina Jacobson, Alison Lucas, Kelley Markley, Joan Margo, Stacey Agin Murray, Kim Pastor, Joelle Shallon, Fern Silvernagle, Standolyn Robertson, Janine Sarna-Jones, Roxanne Shroeder, Marcie Singer, Lisa Sarahson, Lucinda Taterka, Jill Weaver.

To our Web designers and hosts Carol Crespo and Lee Harris at Harris Media for the most extraordinary combination of friendship, talent, and impeccable service in the world.

To my attorney Urban Mulvehill, my accountant Alex Linden, my financial planner, friend, and advocate Lisa LaVecchia, a million thanks.

It takes a village to raise a child, and I am indebted to the circle of parents who have been my close friends, supporters, and teachers of how to parent over the years: Cati Sorra, Liz Ezra and Bill Derman, Susan and Richard Sporer, Amy and Jack Cohen, Marilyn and Joel Duckoff, Valerie Soll, Camille, Peter, Hannah and Zoe Ehrenberg, Judy Wineman.

Many of the people already mentioned have become dear friends. In addition, for their unending friendship, encouragement, and support, I thank Mandy Patinkin and Kathryn Grody, Peter Smith, Cheryl Richardson, Hal and Tracy Denton, Quincy Jones, Mary Bryant, Harriet Wohlgemuth, Rebecca Herschkopf, Gordon Rothman, and Gordon Mehler.

This book was made vibrant by the generous contributions of a very special group of teens: Jena Derman, Rebecca Driesen, Isaac Grody-Patinkin, Gideon Grody-Patinkin, Ellie Lotan, Kyle Lehman, Amanda Rios, Jasmin Rios, Heli Sorra, Eric Sporer, Zane Sterling, and Merieke Sterling. Thank you for sharing your time, your brilliant insights, and your perceptions.

Finally, we'd like to thank all the teens who participated in our survey. Your honesty in sharing your experiences and perceptions of the organizing process was exceedingly helpful, moving, and generous. We hope this book will help you in your efforts to become better organized. Many thanks:

Maggie Acevedo

Adenise Alturas

Jen Analetto

Samantha Anglemyer

Tracy Arnston

Sarah Ashley

Jessica Auxier

Sarah Barham

Jenica Barker

Deanna Bartley

Brittany Bennett

Keyona Battle

Andrea Berning

Annette Betancourt

Bri Bickal

Aaron Blackmor

Marissa Borosky

Simone Box

Inna Brayman

Quirine Bredero

Rhonda G. Brent

Kyla Brown

Heather Brown

Michelle Brown

Jenny A. Bryan

Kristen A. Bryson

Brittany Cannon

Kyle Carone

Casey Chaney

Amanda Clark

Jon Coen

Kathy Corcoran

Kelly Cosgrave

Kristen Cosper

Candice Crabtree

Kelsey Cutler

Elizabeth Deiter

Shelby Dennis

Sarah Dedge

Diane Douglas

Ashley Durrbeck

Raquel Edwards

Jane Everclear

Liz Figueroa

Beecha Filer

Shannon Gammage

Sarah George

Heather Gibson

Ashley Goode

Allison D. Grace

Lizzy Gruner

Kim Gusa

Laura Hagen

Ashley Hamilton

Christina Hammond

Michelle Harn

Whitney Hass

Skyler Haupt

Kristina Holden

Lynn Hurley

Sarah Iverson

Dragana Ivkovic

Heather M. Jennings

Erica Johnson

Amanda Johnson

Andrea Jones

Bailey Kaiser

Kimberly Karwath

Alicia Kennedy

Alyson Kiel

Epiphany A. Kirkwood

Christina Knipling

Heather Lambert

Victoria Lee

Sarah Lisko

Heather Loftis

Stephanie Luff

Kimberly M.

Marie Macher

Corrie Marquardt

Monika Martinez

Cathy Maurizi

Emily May

Shelley McClung

Janet Mendoza

Katrina Mercer

Kathy Mertsock

Adrian Moody

Kody May Moore

Becky L. Moulton

Brandi Nepsa

Cecily Newman

Carrie Nign

Erika Nyborg

Theresa O'Malley

Amber Ortiz

Lakisha Parker

Amanda Paustian

Ashley Preuss

Jennifer Procanik

Gabrielle Qahhar

Stephanie Quesada

Regina Ramcharran

Marieann Ramirez

Caitlyn Randell

Fatima Rangoonwala

Cord Rapert

Rebecca Ratliff

Vanessa Reynolds

Shantel Robinson

Tanisha Robinson

Kayla Robinson

April Rodda

Annette Rodriguez

Eric Rosenstein

Ashley Ryback

Shawnta Santacruz

Jennifer Schooley

Bob Scoggins

Melissa Scott

Debra Sear

Virginia Sellers

Stephanie
   Seonbuchner

Hannah Silva

Melecia Simpson

Christina Singletary
Jennifer Slyter
Jessica Smith
Amber Spillman
Lauren Spindle
Heidi Storm
Lauren Strickland
Melissa Swope
Ann Terry
Sanja Terzic
Ben Thomson
Tiffany Thorne
Joselin Torres
Jean Tracy
Stephanie Vacchio
Marina Vasilyeva
Alesia Walker
Rachel Williams
Elizabeth Wolfe
Stephanie Wonning

Brittany Yamauchi
Kelly Youngblood
Shaunah Zimmerman
Anna Zudell
Kira Swearingen
Emily Westrick
Leah M. J. Westrick
Pamela Androff
Alicia Calvert
Jessica Cottril
Jonathan Cottril
Candice Crabtree
Sean Doerr
Rebecca Driesen
P. Gangolly
Jennifer Gehring
Catherine Geisik
B. Gurecki
Shari Harrington
Lisa Hartmann

Katie Keranen
Casey Kimura
Ellie Lotan
Megan McCourt
Jessica Moore
Isaac Pham
Victoria Pierce
Marieann Ramirez
Emily Resnick
Bernice Santacruz
Rosemary Scianna
Heli Sorra
Katie Tokie
Art Torres
Emma Towle
Stephanie Vacchio
Rebecca Velasco
Jean Watkins
Andrea Week

Marie
Tori
Alyssa
Amanda
Emily
Nicole
Bridgette
Suzanna
Shawna
Jessica
Ashley

Allison
Caitlin
Angele
Kelsey
Tiffany
Chrysayne
Rachel
Amanda
Amanda
Staci
Trista

Kandy
Andrea
Angela
Veronica
Carol
Jade
Crystal
Meggan
Regina
Teresa
Sara

Jessi's

Writing this book has been an exciting and fascinating process. In its creation, there have been several people whose assistance and support have been crucial to the process, as well as crucial to my ability to take on a project of such magnitude.

First and foremost, I'd like to thank Elina and Jennifer, to whom I owe my life for their patience and cooperation as I worked through this book with so many different activities on my plate. Both of your immeasurable innovative contributions have made this book all that it is. Elina, your remarkable strength for structure, and Jennifer, your magnifying glass of an eye have fostered this book to jump off the pages. Thank you so much, as you each have helped me to be a better writer and have a better understanding of this business in so many ways.

My ultimate gratitude to Faith Hamlin for paving the way for this project, and to Joni Evans, who embraced the concept and orchestrated the reality with the hands of a maestro.

A million and one thank yous to Maggie Richards and John Sterling for their continual support and inspiring enthusiasm about this project. Also thank you to Sarah Hutson, Ruth Kaplan, Elizabeth Shreve, and David Sobel for each playing the part of a vertebra in the making and promotion of this book. Tracey Locke, thank you for walking home with me on September 11.

Most importantly, thank you Mom for your decision to write this with me. It has been an astounding, bonding, life-changing experience, and thanks to you, we had fun all the while! I'm so proud of you, and so happy to have had the privilege of working with you side by side.

To the Colón, Morgenstern, and Nell families for being so accommodating and loving in every circumstance. For giving me the space to develop as an individual and for being there when I need you most. Thank you Yady, Clarence, and Len for your company; though we aren't in the closest of contact, I always feel your energy holding me up from behind, and for that I am in the utmost debt to you.

The past sixteen years I have been "snowballing" people into my circle of support and friends. This network provides me with a tremendous amount of focus, confidence, and stamina in achieving even the most minor of goals.

I'd like to take this opportunity to thank everyone from the National Dance Institute, namely Jacques D'Amboise, Lesli Kappel, Ellen Weinstein, Jenny Seham, and Lori Klinger for having given me the gift of finding my passion at such an early age and supporting me continually throughout the development of it. Also to the many friends I have made through NDI whose presence in my life is nothing short of a miracle. Thank you to Erica Litke and John Holcomb for understanding me so thoroughly and being such heartening and loyal friends.

Thank you to all of my teachers at Steps on Broadway for providing me with a challenging and comfortable place to grow and begin to establish myself as a dancer. My deepest appreciation to Jane Miller Gifford, Roberta Mathes, Vicki Fischer, and Jeff Edmond for coaching me and being my mentors in so many ways.

I owe the greatest of thanks to Hashomer Hatzair North America and everyone from Camp Shomria for teaching me to be the best person that I can be. Thank you to all of the Moshava, especially Hatzor for your unfathomable devotion, amity, and reliability in every event. A special thank you to Jonah for being my own personal Dumbledore.

I am extraordinarily lucky to be at a school where I can grow in so many directions at once. Thank you to all of my teachers who have supported and fostered my love for learning throughout the past five years. To Sheila Breslaw, Rob Menken, and Wendy Muskat for being so dedicated to us as a student body, as well as each of us as individuals. A very special thanks to Brooke Jackson and Nelly Valentin for their encouragement, shared knowledge, insight, and friendship.

To every single person in the class of 2003 at the NYC Lab School for teaching me about the many different forms of friendship. To my close circle of friends that has rallied around me in every high and low: Stephanie, Sarah, Rachel, Lilly, Jessica, Casey, Nina, Lena, Alisa, and Serena. Sarah and Lilly, thank you for helping me to keep up with school during the various stages of this book. Stephanie, thank you for being my soul sister.

Thank you to Jed Bernstein, whose companionship unendingly has been the motivation to be myself, and for being the best kind of friend anyone could ever ask for.

And finally, thank you to my marvelous, noble, powerhouse of a Papi. I look forward to nothing more than Wednesday nights, when I get my recharging of energy and newly sparked wisdom from the bottomless sage. You have been the rock-solid base in my life for every dream I've ever had, and you have pushed me to reach every one of them. Your belief in me has given me everything I need to continue to make you proud.

Julie Morgenstern is the founder and cofounder of the professional organizing firm TASK MASTERS, and the author of the *New York Times* best-seller *Organizing from the Inside Out* and *Time Management from the Inside Out*. Since 1989, Julie and her staff have helped people who want to get organized and companies who want to do more in less time.

As a speaker, media expert, and corporate spokesperson, Julie is known for her engaging, articulate style, and warm sense of humor. She is a regular columnist for *O, The Oprah Magazine,* solving readers' problems by helping to "tame the chaos" in their lives. Julie has also been a guest on many TV and radio shows, including *The Oprah Show, Today, Good Morning America,* and National Public Radio. She is quoted and featured regularly in a wide variety of publications including *The New York Times, The Chicago Tribune, Women's Day, Health Magazine, Cosmopolitan, Shape,* and *McCall's.*

Organizing from the Inside Out has been made into a popular PBS Video Special. Her books are available in audio versions and have been translated into many different languages. Julie demystifies the process of getting organized by making it simple, do-able, and fun.

A noted leader in the professional organizing industry, Julie has served on the Board of Directors and as the National Expo Chair and National Associate Member Chair of the National Association of Professional Organizers (NAPO). She was honored with the prestigious Founders Award, presented by the National Association of Professional Organizers, in 2002. Julie is also a member of the National Speakers Association (NSA).

Julie's background in the theater as a director, producer, and performer provides the foundation for her work as an organizer. She believes organizing requires the same set of skills as directing/producing—an appreciation of spatial design, the ability to see the big picture as well as the tiny details, and the talent to blend psychology and practical skills to guide people where they want to go.

Her education includes a BA in theater from Temple University and study at the Directing Program at Goodman School of Drama.

Jessi Morgenstern-Colón is sixteen years old. She is a student, dancer, activist, journalist, and writer. A junior this year, Jessi will graduate from high school in June 2003.

Jessi's passions are her dancing and writing. She began dancing with the National Dance Institute at the age of three and now trains with Steps on Broadway. She has appeared on the *Today* show and Nickelodeon and performed twice at the White House. Jessi has also contributed her writing and editorial skills to several teen Web sites and newspapers, including Hipo.com, where she has written reviews on clothing, celebrities, and television shows, and *New Youth Connections*, where she has contributed feature articles geared toward urban youth.

Jessi aspires to be a professional dancer for as long as she is able. She then plans to become a high school English teacher, while continuing to pursue and explore her interests in creative writing and reporting. In her spare time, she enjoys Rollerblading, youth leadership activities, and traveling; she's also an avid student of languages and the *art* of comfort.

Julie and Jessi live in New York City with the two best cats on the planet, Shadow and Pepper.